LINGERING IN MY HEART

World War II Photographs and Letters

VIRGIL D. HAYNES

EDITED BY CYNTHIA A. HAYNES

INTRODUCTION BY EDWARD F. REUTER

HAYNES STUDIO, PUBLISHERS

ACKNOWLEDGMENTS AND NOTES

I would like to thank my father, Virgil D. Haynes, for his innate sense of insight and artistry. He truly *felt* the story behind what may have seemed to others, merely common everyday events. This book contains selected images from his many photographs and excerpts from his letters, description lists and handwritten chronologies detailing his U.S. Army experiences.

It should be noted that those photographic captions quoted directly from his photographic description lists (which had been sent home along with groupings of small photos he had made) are found in italic print beside certain images.

The letter excerpts, some transcribed and some in his own hand, reflect the fact that mail was strictly censored. Soldiers were not allowed to discuss any military matters or give their location until *after* a country was liberated. Remember, too, that those in service often kept letters a bit "cheerier" than events and situations actually may have been so as not to alarm loved ones at home in the States.

I also acknowledge, with thanks, the personal faith of my father, his roots generationally deep in the Church of the Brethren, and his strong commitment to his wife, Audrey Haynes, to whom he wrote these letters. And, I thank the inspiring and patriotic servicemen and women of the U.S. Army 38th Station Hospital for their courage and hard work while in the difficult circumstances of World War II. I have had the privilege of knowing many of them and witnessing the depth of their lifelong and loyal friendships. Their members met in various towns and cities across the U.S. for a total of twenty reunions, the last in 1999.

–C.A.H.

P.O. Box 383
Harbor Springs, Michigan 49740
U.S.A.

First Edition, *released in September 2005, to commemorate the 60th Anniversary of the end of World War II.*

Library of Congress Control Number: 2005928649

ISBN-13: 978-0-9623243-2-1
ISBN-10: 0-9623243-2-9

Editing and conceptual: Cynthia A. Haynes, Haynes Studio
Page design and layout: Laura Cherven, Sage Designworks

Printed by: Mitchell Graphics, Inc., Petoskey, Michigan

PRINTED IN THE UNITED STATES OF AMERICA

OPPOSITE Photograph of Virgil D. Haynes taken in the Smoky Mountains by Audrey Haynes on a trip to Florida, just prior to his U.S. Army induction, early March, 1942

Sergeant Ed Reuter at his desk with pictures of Lorraine, his wife, Chartres, 1945

INTRODUCTION

A quiet man, articulate, witty and, above all, meticulous; not a tall man, but a man who *stood tall*—that's Virgil Haynes. Like most of his generation, Virgil D. Haynes served in World War II. Assigned to the Army Medical Corps, young inductee Haynes trained in first-aid and clinical care, quickly earning the position of Ward Master with the rank of Staff Sergeant. His duties entailed maintaining a duty roster, monitoring performance, coaching where needed, as well as acting as liaison between his "charges" and the professional staff.

As part of the United States Army 38th Station Hospital, Virgil Haynes and fellow soldiers were shipped overseas to provide hospital care for American troops stationed in proximity to the English Channel, troops who were already in training for the liberation of France from German occupation. Some twenty months later, with the anticipated invasion at last underway, battle casualties from the sands of Normandy were ferried across the channel and brought through the doors of our medical unit. The wounded kept coming, were treated, then transferred elsewhere. The pace was unremitting, yet went smoothly, largely due to the 38th's excellent leadership and vigilant hard work such as that exemplified by S/Sgt. Haynes. Concurrent with the Allies' big push inland, the 38th Station Hospital unit followed the advancing forces into France where it would remain until the conflict's end. Upon victory in Europe, and then with the September 2, 1945, formal Japanese surrender ending the war, soldiers could not easily contain their joyful thoughts of going home, yet memories of a fallen brother or buddy prompted solemn visits to cemeteries in France. Nurses, too, would go to gravesites, tear-filled eyes obscuring the markers of those they knew, dated and loved. Walking between the rows and rows of white crosses, we saw more than just the names of those who died. We remembered living, vibrant personalities and were made grimly aware of how many would *not* be going home.

The 38th Station Hospital had been activated July 20, 1942, at Camp Barkeley, hastily constructed in the hot, dusty, barren cattle-country near Abilene, Texas. It was inactivated February 22, 1946, one day following its return to the States. The unit was fortunate to have acquired individuals who led by example and professionals willing to impart their skills. Those characteristics promoted a spirit of cooperation and pride in a job well done. S/Sgt. Haynes was a vital part of this effective and dedicated team.

S/Sgt. Virgil Haynes was married, and faithfully so. Imagine, if you will, that for more than three years, his sole communication home was the written letter. There were certainly many lonely moments; however, to fill his off-duty hours, he pursued his passion for photography. His enthusiasm, patience and penchant for attention to even the smallest detail served him well on his venture into the photographic world. As you read and view the following pages, you will find his personality shining through in each and every letter and photograph.

A fellow soldier and friend,
Edward F. Reuter
Staff Sergeant, United States Army 38th Station Hospital
Served July 4, 1942, to December 1, 1945

38th Station Hospital
17 March 1944
England

My dear Audrey,

Yes, it was just two (2) years ago this morning that you and I left our apartment and started for the bus that was to take me to Camp Custer. As I went out the door I kind of glanced around and tried to catch a quick look at all our things without drawing your attention to what I was doing... the cute little dinette with all those pretty shiny dishes, that favorite platform rocker, the little ivory radio... I can recall how proud we were to have our folks and friends stop over for an evening chat. But then dear, I miss you a bit more than anything. How a fellow misses everything after being away for two years. These are precious pictures I have in my mind that are dear to me and lingering in my heart.

Lovingly from Virgil

ABOVE "Lingering in My Heart" letter written March 17, 1944, Winchester, England

OPPOSITE Audrey Haynes in the kitchen of their Detroit apartment shortly after marriage in 1940 to Virgil D. Haynes

March 17, 1942

Left Detroit, Michigan by bus to Fort Custer

March 23, 1942

Left Fort Custer, Michigan by troop train

March 26, 1942

Arrived at Fort Bliss, Texas

June 26, 1942

Transferred to: 1852 Medical Detachment
Station Hospital
Fort Bliss

July 20, 1942

Transferred to: 38th Station Hospital
Camp Barkeley, Texas

March 18, 1942

We arrived here about 11:15 a.m. yesterday and were taken directly to the Induction Bldg. There we were examined again physically and then had to take the Army oath. At that point I became a "U.S. Soldier."

We were then taken to the warehouse and stripped of our clothes and outfitted with Army duds. I received the following: 1 pair shoes, size 8-D, 3 pair woolen socks, 3 pair underwear, 2 ties, 4 shirts, 4 hankies, complete suit, raincoat, overcoat and gloves and a canteen set. I am to receive yet some towels and a shaving set as an electric shaver is practically useless. I will probably be sending my civilian clothes home soon but can keep my brown shoes and wear them on my own time.

Now I'm feeling well, but my eating isn't like it was at my mother's or your mother's or at our home. However, I'll get adjusted sooner or later. I've got to expect a lot of this, but coming from such a good home, it is just a little hard to take. It really is a complete change, but I presume it could be much worse.

Say hello to all the folks and friends and thank them for the lovely little notes they gave me when I left. It does my heart good to read them, and I know that they realize what a sacrifice we must go through. I'm sure that God is hearing their prayers, as well as mine, and I continue to pray that this thing will end and we may see and be with each other soon. Keep your chin up and everything will come out all right.

March 19, 1942

Here I am again, and as you can see, I'm still able to write. Ha.Ha. I am the only one in the barracks right now, oh, except one fellow here who is from Cadillac, Mich. He would be out with the other guys, too, but I guess he's broke. So far the only money I've spent is for my phone call to you, a Coca-Cola, a Detroit newspaper and the latest edition of *Popular Photo*.

We had our first of a series of shots in the arm. One in the right and one in the left. Then we had to eat and put on our K.P. (Kitchen Police) clothes that are for doing dirty work. We are able to keep ourselves quite clean and have showers. Oh, and today I shaved with the safety razor they gave me and it felt like I was tearing my whole face apart! We are able to have mustaches, but they try to have the boys do away with them as much as possible. How do you think I'd look with a mustache and no hair?

March 26, 1942

We arrived here at Fort Bliss a short time ago after spending 3 nights and 2 days on the train. We did not set foot on ground until we reached Texas. We were confined to a few cars. Just as we left Custer, the USO Ladies gave us magazines, fruit, candy, cards, envelopes and pencils. We knew then that we were going for a long, long train ride.

We are to start our drilling and training this coming Monday. Gee, they certainly are getting the fellows into the Army—large, small, fat and skinny and old and young and many with all sorts of things wrong.

I believe God has his hand over the two of us so that we are able to see each other again soon, and I pray for help and guidance and for Him to intervene between men so that this war will stop, and that we may all come back to our loved ones.

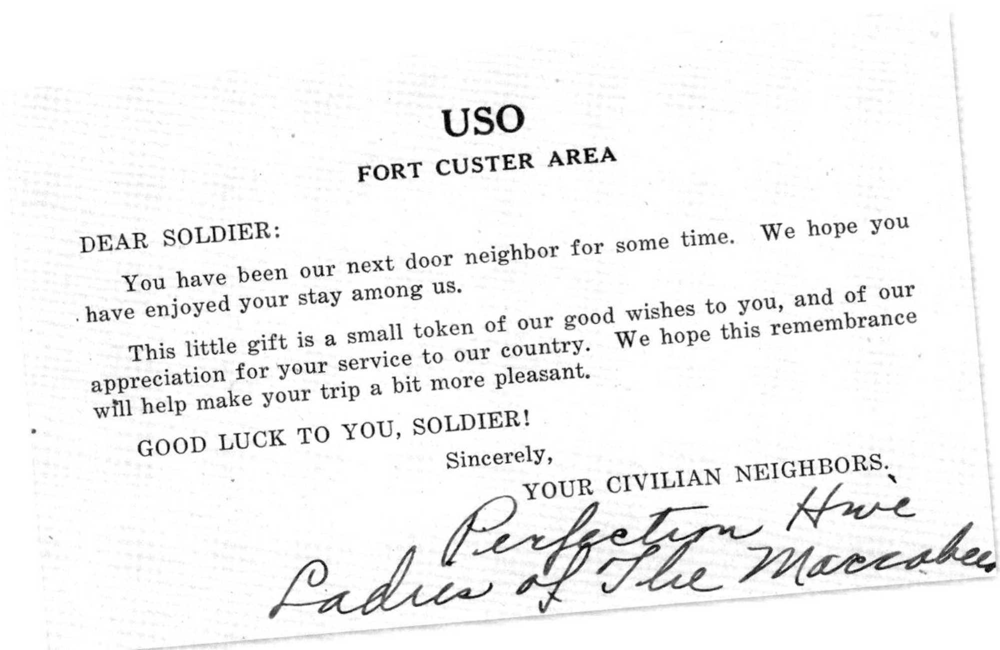

USO

FORT CUSTER AREA

DEAR SOLDIER:

You have been our next door neighbor for some time. We hope you have enjoyed your stay among us.

This little gift is a small token of our good wishes to you, and of our appreciation for your service to our country. We hope this remembrance will help make your trip a bit more pleasant.

GOOD LUCK TO YOU, SOLDIER!

Sincerely,

YOUR CIVILIAN NEIGHBORS.

Perfection Hive
Ladies of The Maccabees

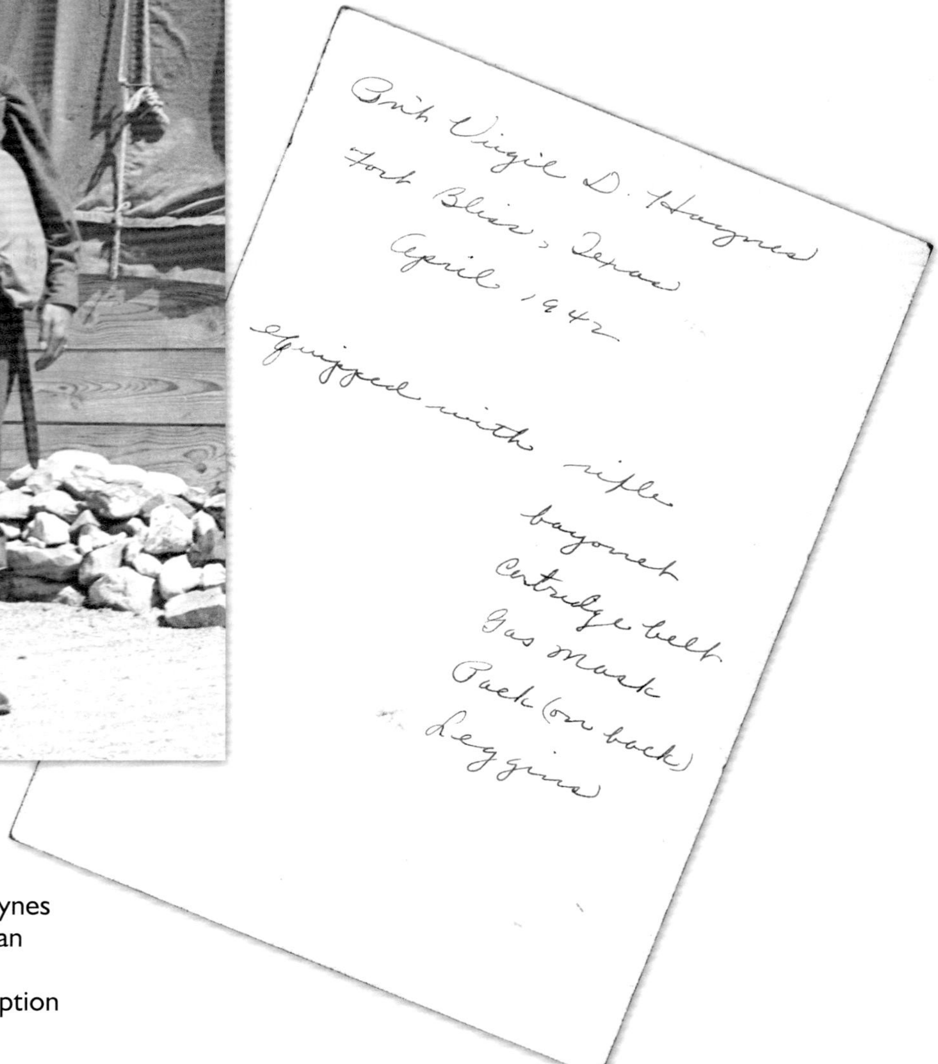

Photograph of Virgil D. Haynes snapped on his camera by an army buddy or by his own delayed shutter, and description from back of photo, 1942

March 28, 1942

I still haven't received any mail here yet…I know it takes time. I'll be looking for a letter from you soon, and when I get it I'll be the most joyful guy in camp. The first day here was no good at all because the more I thought how far away from home I was, the more it hurt. But, I'm feeling fine now and getting used to the country here. I can sort of forget about it being so barren and desolate, and I feel God is near all the time when I look in any direction and see His handiwork in the mountains. Our tent faces north and the mountains are west. This is the way the top outline of the mountains are looking from our tent grounds:

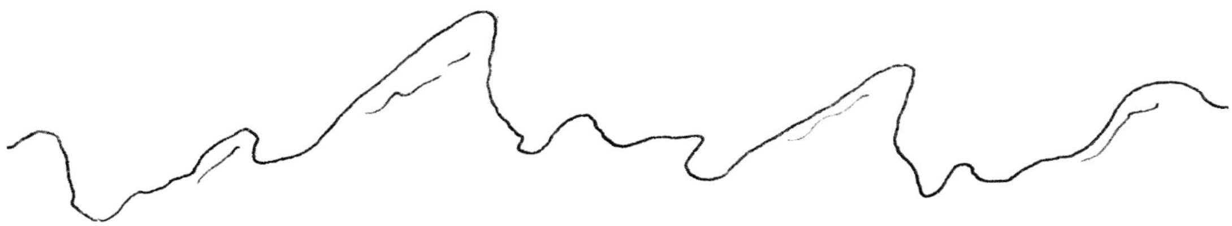

After I look at them a while, I feel that there is beauty to them after all. The weather is rather nice, too. We live in tents, and they really aren't quite as bad as I had expected. The tent is about 16 or 17 feet square, has a wooden floor and base and then the top part is tenting. There are only five in our tent and it makes it nicer that way than all together in one big barrack like at Fort Custer.

Inside tent at
Fort Bliss, Texas, 1942

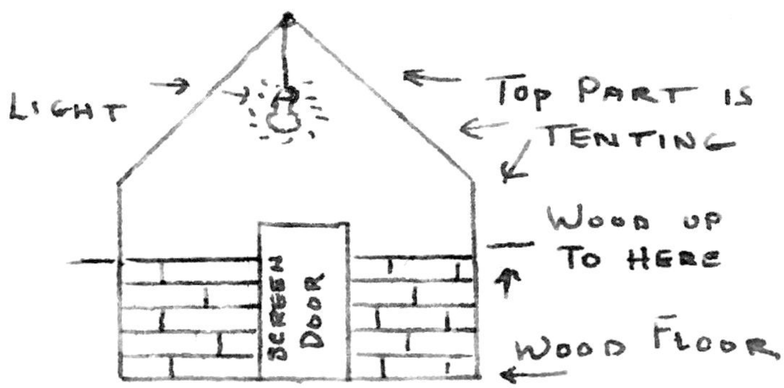

April 4, 1942

Boy, the mail sure did come in the past two days…now I have five letters and a telegram from you. I received a package of chocolates and a can of potato chips from my family and your box of goodies—you sure know what I like, and the nuts in the bottom of the box were a big surprise. The fellows in my tent said they sure were glad I was in this particular tent!

April 10, 1942

We just now came back from the drill field and all batteries were drilling and marching to the band music. We had a 45-min. class on rifle cleaning, too. We will no doubt get to bed early as we must make another 10-mile hike tomorrow. This time we are staying out all day and coming back in the early eve. Before that, we had a 10-mile hike with our packs. Each man has half of a pup tent plus we must take our raincoats, blanket, toilet articles, canteen and mess kit and a few other things. It is quite heavy, but then, we strong men can take it. It's beginning to get warm here. Yesterday it was 88 and we were out in the desert with no shade. We hike out into the desert nearby, put up our tents, display all our equipment for the Colonel and then pack it all up and put it on our backs and march back. Oh well, it's the shoes that belong to "Uncle Sam" that I'm wearing out.

We now have six in our tent, and the last chap brought an R.C.A. Victor battery and electric radio. We listen to it quite a bit and get the news and some favorite evening programs. The fellows in my tent are Pvt. Rasey from Oklahoma, a tall lanky lad, age 22 and single, Pvt. Brennan from Wisconsin, age 29, tall and slender, dark-haired and single, Pvt. Kedickle from Detroit, age 23, married only 6-weeks and very much in love, Pvt. Kern from Detroit, 31 and single. He is a lot of fun all the time. Pvt. King is from Bay City, Mich., was a commercial fisherman on Saginaw Bay, is 25 and single. A very nice fellow as they are all. We all get along fine and have a lot of good times. Then there's Pvt. Virgil D. Haynes from Detroit. He is 27 and very much married, and still in love a lot. He goes to church, is dark-skinned with a high and shiny forehead but is still the best lookin' one in the tent! Ha.Ha.

Marching at
Fort Bliss, Texas, 1942

October 11, 1942

Left Camp Barkeley, Texas by troop train

October 14, 1942

Arrived in Camp Kilmer, New Jersey

October 19, 1942

Left Camp Kilmer, Boarded "Mariposa"
New York Harbor

October 20, 1942

Sailed from New York

October 28, 1942

Arrived Liverpool, England

October 29, 1942

Troop train to West Bromich

November 11, 1942

Arrived at Winchester, England

SPECIAL PASS TO "E" DECK OF TROOP SHIP "MARIPOSA" 5500 TROOPS ON BOARD. TRAVELED ALONE – 9 DAYS – 9-NIGHTS

THE WHITE HOUSE
WASHINGTON

TO MEMBERS OF THE UNITED STATES ARMY EXPEDITIONARY FORCES:

You are a soldier of the United States Army.

You have embarked for distant places where the war is being fought.

Upon the outcome depends the freedom of your lives: the freedom of the lives of those you love—your fellow-citizens—your people.

Never were the enemies of freedom more tyrannical, more arrogant, more brutal.

Yours is a God-fearing, proud, courageous people, which, throughout its history, has put its freedom under God before all other purposes.

We who stay at home have our duties to perform—duties owed in many parts to you. You will be supported by the whole force and power of this Nation. The victory you win will be a victory of all the people—common to them all.

You bear with you the hope, the confidence, the gratitude and the prayers of your family, your fellow-citizens, and your President—

Franklin D Roosevelt

November 5, 1942

Greetings to you from across the Atlantic. Our voyage was quite an event in itself, and of course, a new kind of experience. I had no sea sickness and was O.K. all the time. I am well and feeling fine and dandy and making the best of everything. As for our location—all we can say so far, is that we are in England and the land of the blackout. And I do mean blackout. This is quite a bad rainy night and really pitch black. At the present, I'm inside in the warmth by the fireplace and checking my guard detail. I'm Sgt. of the Guard and so, of course, am busy during the night. My sinus trouble bothers me every now and then but is not too bad. Most everyone has to get used to this climate. We are in a rather quaint old setting among the hills, and it is the perfect picture of England.

The 38th Station Hospital (formerly St. Swithun's School for Girls), Winchester, England, 1942

A picture like this of the Old Chesil Rectory is the very thing that makes England so pretty. This is a typical English building where we can stop in for some tea. These small scenes add up to the fact that the country looks quaint and old. By the way, the bus is on the wrong side of the street, but that is due to the fact that he just came out of a garage. The ladies on horses are American nurses from another hospital nearby. Winchester, 1942

EDITOR'S NOTE

Photographic captions quoted directly from Virgil D. Haynes' descriptive lists or which were handwritten on the backs of photographs are found in italic print.

Here's a scene of the river Itchen near what's called "the Meadows." This is really one of the nicest and most peaceful views I know. Winchester, 1942

Left to right: George Lunceford, Virgil Haynes, H.E. "Gene" Reneau, Sylvester "Bud" Dressen and Bruce Hull during a visit of the Red Cross coffee and donut wagon. I set the camera on the tripod and used delayed motion but had a tough time getting seated so my pose looks a little funny. Winchester, 1942

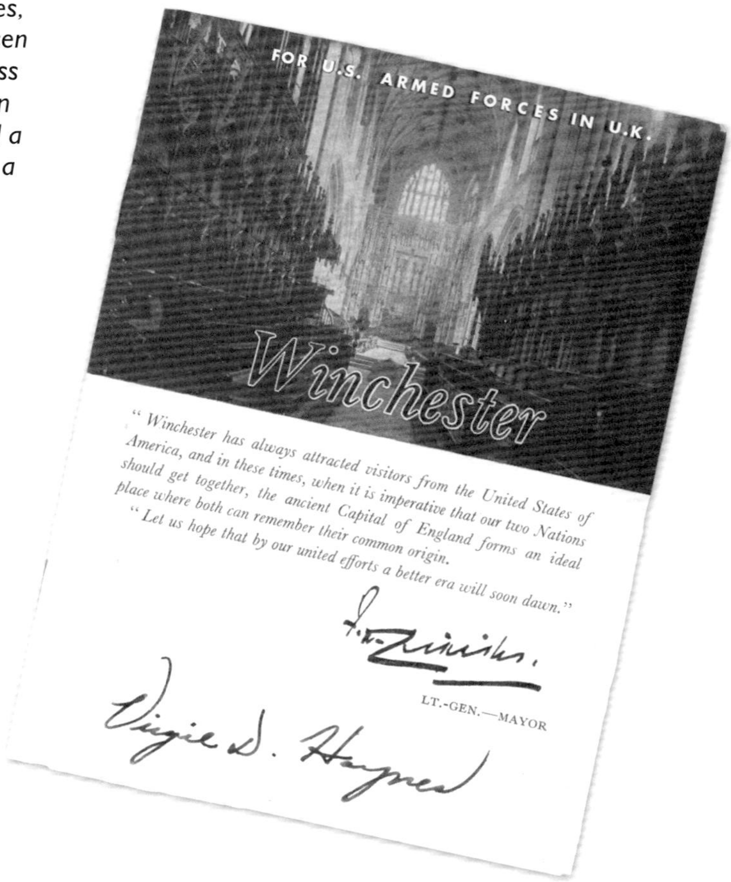

Ellie Knaack, Anne Bernhardt and Mary Dobroski enjoying donuts and coffee in front of the 38th Station Hospital. Winchester, 1942

Shadowed street and bicycle rider in Winchester, 1942

ABOVE AND BELOW *This is the hill that we have to go up and down in order to go from the post to the town and back. It really is steeper than the camera seems to record.* Winchester, 1942

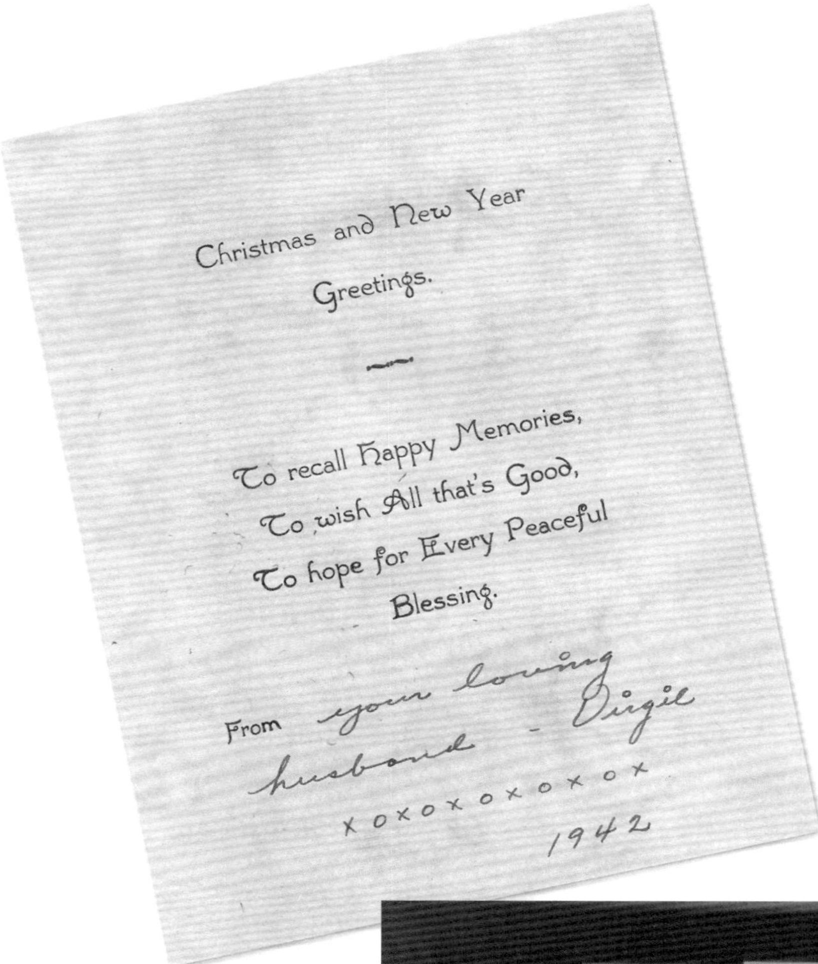

Christmas and New Year
Greetings.

To recall Happy Memories,
To wish All that's Good,
To hope for Every Peaceful
Blessing.

From your loving
husband – Virgil
xoxoxoxoxox
1942

BELOW Auditorium Stage of the 38th Station Hospital at Christmastime, Winchester, 1942

Here is one of the nicest photographs I have taken so far, I think. This is the door to Easton Church that I have gone through several times when I went to services. It's across from the family I met, the Heathcotes. Near Winchester, 1943

March 10, 1943

It was one year ago this time that we were on vacation in Miami enjoying ourselves very much. This was brought back to my mind again last Sunday as I was in the Miami of England. Cpl. Hull and I had a pass over Saturday and Sunday, so we put our bikes and ourselves on a fast train to Bournemouth on the sea. It was quite a thrill to see the ocean once more, and that alone brought back happy memories of many things in Miami. The hotels all overlook the water and are the same styles and colors as in Miami. The streets are well-paved and wide, the houses are very new and modern—we just rode and rode for miles along the edge of the bluff. I could forget for a day that a war was going on, and as we sat there overlooking the sea, one could hardly realize that just some miles away were people whom we are at war with. It just didn't seem possible. One family came by, and I couldn't help but notice that the father had his pipe and newspaper, mother had her sewing, the little boy had a book to read and the little girl had her baby doll along. They seemed to be having a good time even under the present conditions.

Getting directions along the way, England, 1943

A popular beach at Bournemouth, 1943

Sightseeing soldiers view outdoor art at Bournemouth beach, 1943

March 20, 1943

The Army boys are here getting footage for their movies and taking "stills." Today, Cpl. Hull and I were photographed outside on our bikes to show just how we make our bike trips. The photos were taken with a Speed Graphic and with the clouds as a background should make for some very fine prints. I'll send you a copy soon. The classification that the War Dept. puts these pictures in will determine whether you or we see them in newsreels, magazines or ads or any other way that the Army wants to show the "Medical Soldier."

ABOVE Photograph of Hull and Haynes taken by unknown Army photographer, Winchester, 1943

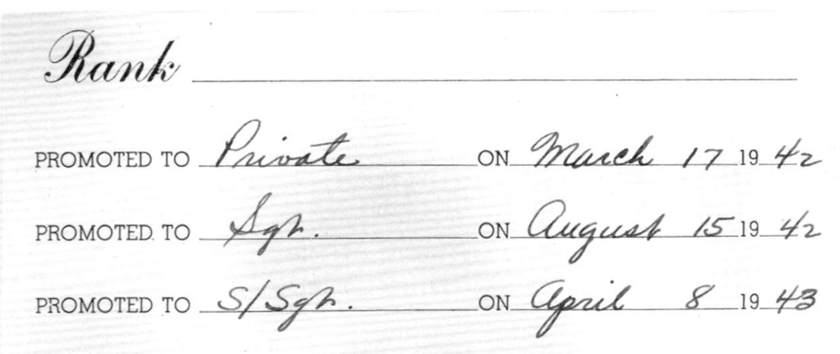

Rank ______________________

PROMOTED TO Private ON March 17 1942

PROMOTED TO Sgt. ON August 15 1942

PROMOTED TO S/Sgt. ON April 8 1943

The road to Easton was always my favorite trail. This is typical of the thatched roof cottages, and I do think they look so pretty. Now that this picture is finished, I see where I could have improved it much more. Anyhow, I like it and will always remember this place. Near Winchester, 1943

April 25, 1943

At long last I am getting some pictures to you. I certainly do think that they are pretty good and hope that you and the folks can get a little idea of our hospital outfit and of our bike rides. I have a really nice bike. Right now it is all oiled-up for our trip to Scotland and around. Think of me when you see a "Yank" on a bike, O.K.? In fact, I'm planning on a little bike ride someplace today. The cathedral bells are ringing again and are so pretty.

LEFT Boy on the train to Scotland, 1943

Edinburgh Castle, Scotland, 1943

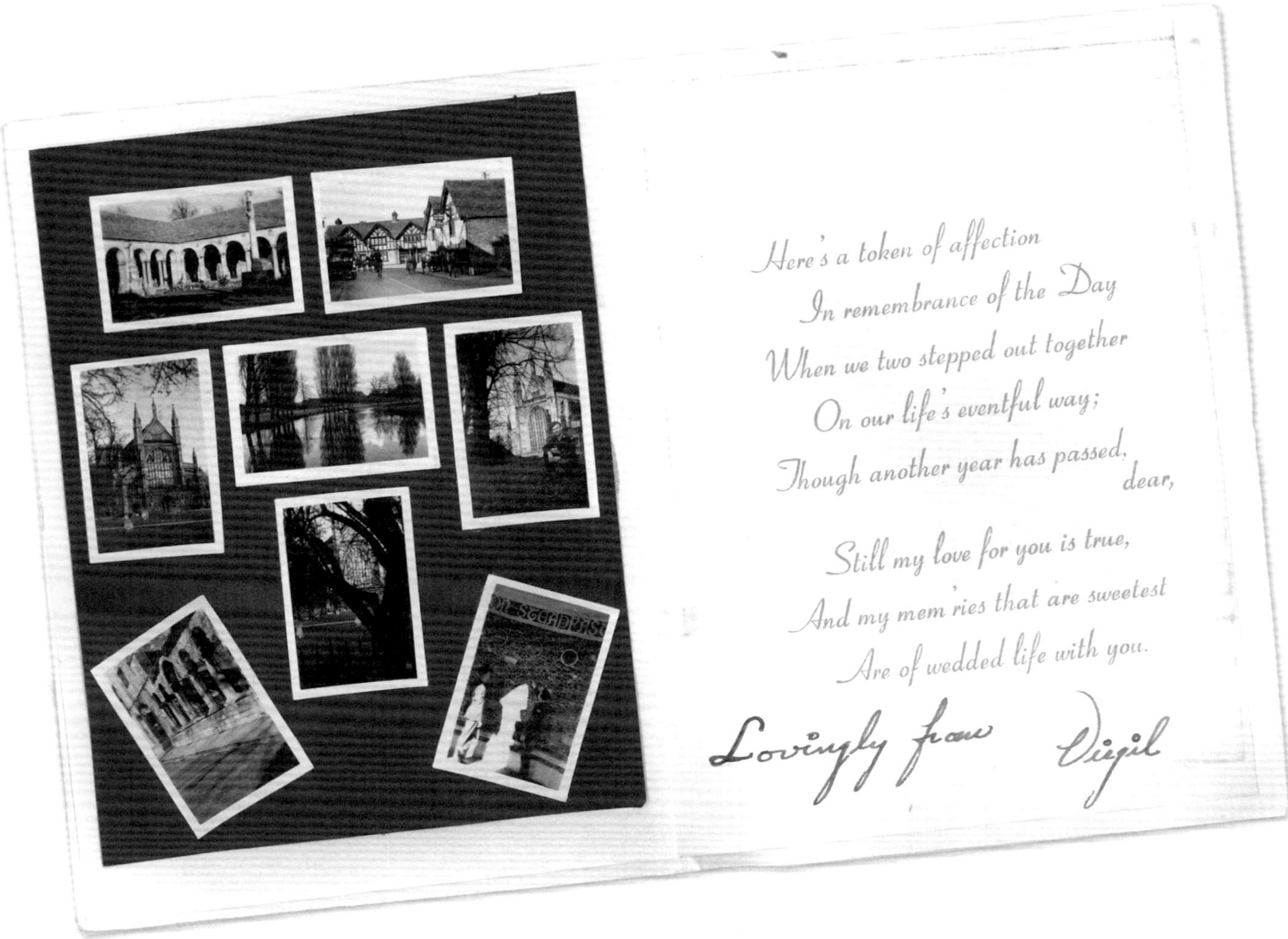

ABOVE Anniversary card with small handmade proof sheet sent in May for third wedding anniversary, June 1, 1943

OPPOSITE *Being able to photograph such a beautiful cathedral seems like a dream to me. Truly, I think the cathedral has been the most important thing to me...I could go there as many times as possible, and each time, just stand and admire its beauty.* Sgt. Lunceford silhouetted against Winchester Cathedral, 1943

June 5, 1943

I went through my bags the other day, and in the process of house-cleaning, I found that I still had the small booklet on our Voigtlander, so I'm sending it home to you to keep with the camera. Also thought I'd send the booklet for the 35mm Agfa I'm using so you can see just what it's like. I don't think I'll need it, so just put it away with our other photo things. I'm really very much pleased with it.

College boys fencing, Winchester, 1943

Here's a little picture for you. We're still working, eating, sleeping, and sightseeing. London, 1943

On a Sunday afternoon along the Itchen River. Winchester, 1943

June 27, 1943

Your V-mail letter came to me this morning following church services, and indeed, I was shocked to hear the sad news about Ken. I pray that it may be a mistake, but as a rule, they are seldom made. I often wondered where Ken might have been, not hearing from him for some time. I have just written the Gordons a letter and tried to express to them that Ken really wouldn't mind giving his life because he had a mission to do. And, speaking for myself, I feel the same way. Many thoughts seem to change after being in certain situations and having certain obligations to fulfill. We just seem to get that way. It's just in the line of duty. In the last letter I received from Ken, he wrote,

"I know you will agree that we receive a lot of inspiration and fortitude from all the good Christian people we know. It's really something to know there are so many real people behind us. Until next time, be good and remember our common source of strength in time of trouble."

I don't want you and the folks to worry about me. We take every precaution against air raids, and it certainly does give us a sense of security. We keep well on the alert, and each man knows just what he is to do and what is expected of him. Anyone with a keen mind and a level head will pull through O.K. We soldiers don't think about danger, but when danger comes, we are prepared. Be brave and don't give up hope. Keep that chin up, just like you have...all will come out well.

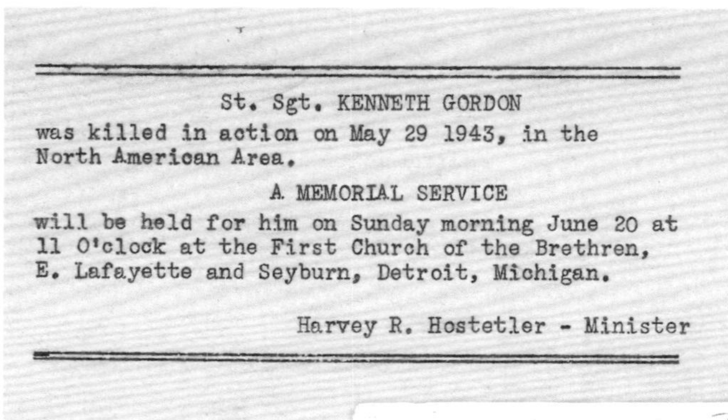

St. Sgt. KENNETH GORDON
was killed in action on May 29 1943, in the North American Area.

A MEMORIAL SERVICE
will be held for him on Sunday morning June 20 at 11 O'clock at the First Church of the Brethren, E. Lafayette and Seyburn, Detroit, Michigan.

Harvey R. Hostetler - Minister

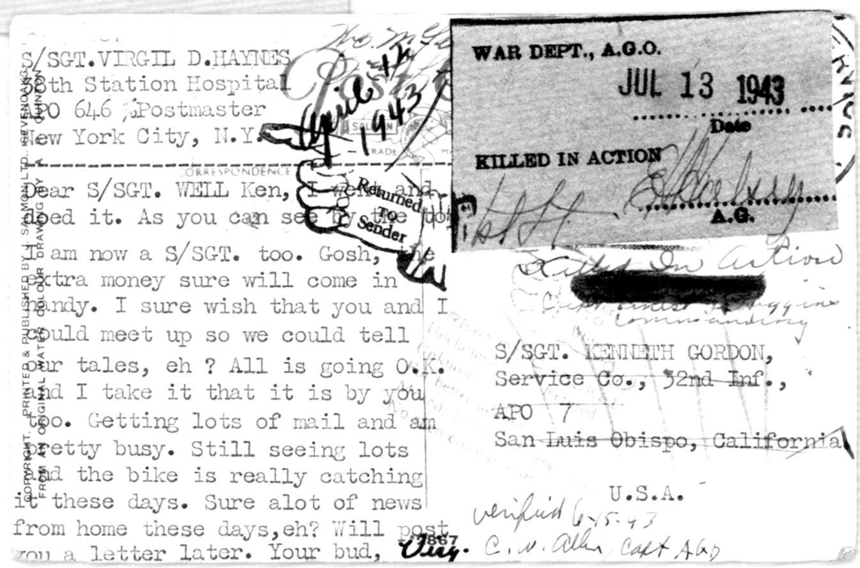

S/SGT. VIRGIL D. HAYNES
38th Station Hospital
APO 646 c/o Postmaster
New York City, N.Y.

Dear S/SGT. WELL Ken, I went and doed it. As you can see by the top I am now a S/SGT. too. Gosh, the extra money sure will come in handy. I sure wish that you and I could meet up so we could tell our tales, eh ? All is going O.K. and I take it that it is by you too. Getting lots of mail and am pretty busy. Still seeing lots and the bike is really catching it these days. Sure alot of news from home these days, eh? Will post you a letter later. Your bud, Virg.

Returned to Sender

WAR DEPT., A.G.O.
JUL 13 1943
Date
KILLED IN ACTION
A.G.

Killed in action

S/SGT. KENNETH GORDON,
Service Co., 32nd Inf.,
APO 7
San Luis Obispo, California
U.S.A.

verified 6-15-43
C. W. Allen Capt AGD

Staff Sergeant Ken Gordon with his mother and father, Netta and Walter Gordon, on one of his last visits home, Detroit, late 1941

July 22, 1943

On July 20th, we celebrated the one year anniversary of the "38th." Col. Becker gave a little speech and brought back a lot of memories, some pleasant and some not so pleasant. The menu was pretty good, and everything looked nice. We sure do appreciate meals like that. Then, the enlisted men had their dance in the auditorium which lasted until 12:30. We had NCOs volunteer for K.P., and so, of course, I helped on that. All I want to do is K.P. for you, again, dear! I hope you have been enjoying the snaps I have been sending, and that you can get some idea of the English countryside. I went to town this afternoon with Cpl. Chiapelli and we saw the picture "Springtime in the Rockies." It was very pretty and a good story. The Technicolor was superb. Some English women behind us always went "Ah" and "Oh" as all the beautiful scenes were flashed on the screen. We also saw the invasion of Sicily on the newsreel. Then we came back and played badminton in the auditorium.

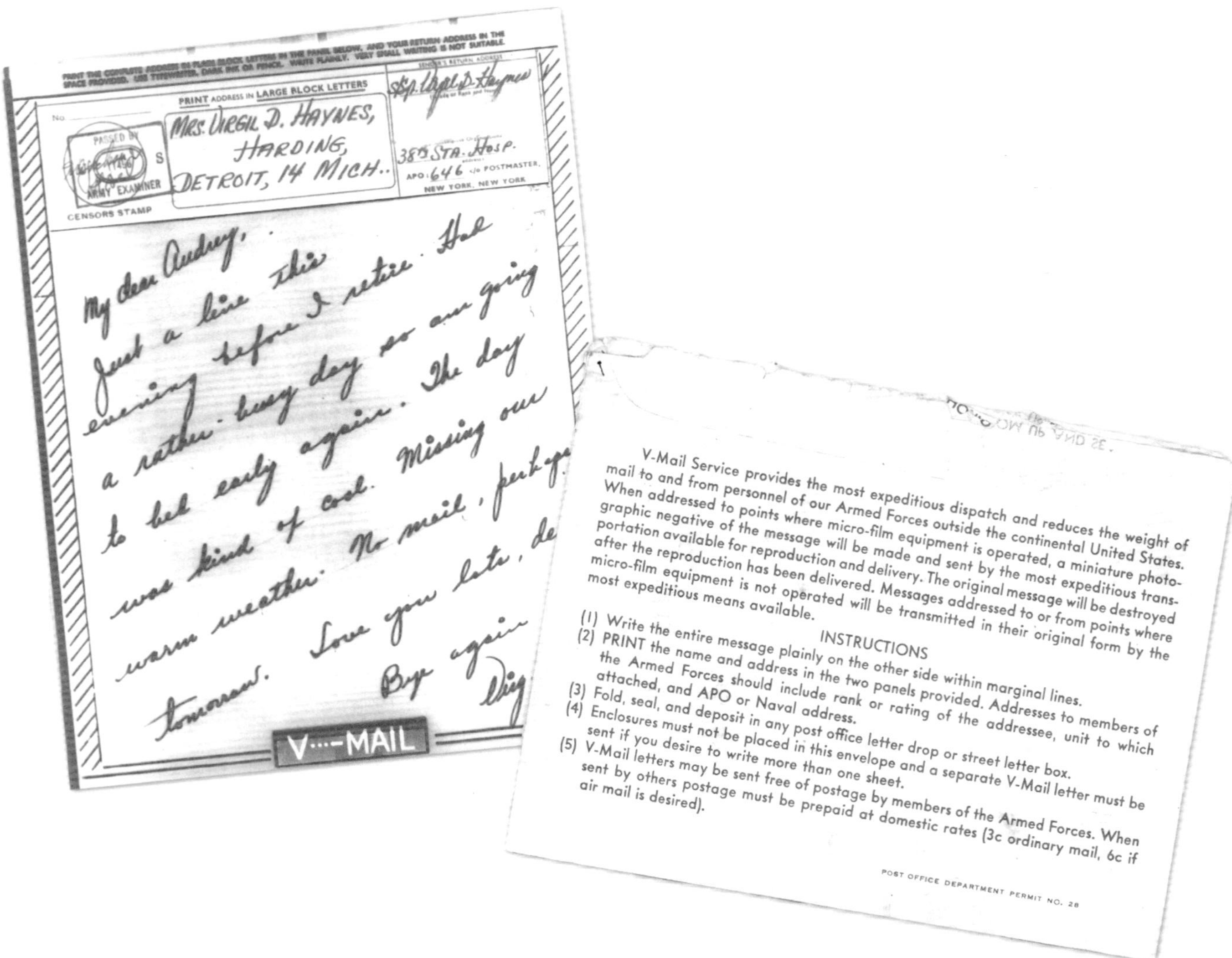
PRINT ADDRESS IN LARGE BLOCK LETTERS

MRS. VIRGIL D. HAYNES,
HARDING,
DETROIT, 14 MICH..

PASSED BY ARMY EXAMINER

CENSORS STAMP

38th STA. HOSP.
APO 646 c/o POSTMASTER,
NEW YORK, NEW YORK

My dear Audrey,

Just a line this evening before I retire. Had a rather busy day so am going to bed early again. The day was kind of cool. Missing our warm weather. No mail, perhaps tomorrow. Love you lots, de

Bye again
Virg

V---MAIL

V-Mail Service provides the most expeditious dispatch and reduces the weight of mail to and from personnel of our Armed Forces outside the continental United States. When addressed to points where micro-film equipment is operated, a miniature photographic negative of the message will be made and sent by the most expeditious transportation available for reproduction and delivery. The original message will be destroyed after the reproduction has been delivered. Messages addressed to or from points where micro-film equipment is not operated will be transmitted in their original form by the most expeditious means available.

INSTRUCTIONS

(1) Write the entire message plainly on the other side within marginal lines.
(2) PRINT the name and address in the two panels provided. Addresses to members of the Armed Forces should include rank or rating of the addressee, unit to which attached, and APO or Naval address.
(3) Fold, seal, and deposit in any post office letter drop or street letter box.
(4) Enclosures must not be placed in this envelope and a separate V-Mail letter must be sent if you desire to write more than one sheet.
(5) V-Mail letters may be sent free of postage by members of the Armed Forces. When sent by others postage must be prepaid at domestic rates (3c ordinary mail, 6c if air mail is desired).

POST OFFICE DEPARTMENT PERMIT NO. 28

Ball game at the 38th Station Hospital, Winchester, 1943

From the *Bars and Stripes*, *The Unit News*, July, 1943

SOFTBALL

The race for championship of the Twilight League is tighter than was expected; 3 teams now being tied for first place.

The "Bums" or the "Jockeys are the likely champs, with the "Sad-Sacks" as a definite threat. The Cut-Ups have finished their schedule dropping 3 out of 5 games and appear to be out of the running. The Buck Passers have had a rough time in their last two games but may rally and upset one of the favorites. As for the Termites, they may still be a bug in anyone's ear.

EVENT OF THE WEEK

For the past two days, this unit has been honored by a visit from 12 soldiers representing the Educational Department of the British Army. This visit was made to create a better understanding between the American and British Armies; so that we may both understand the politics, home life, and scruples of each nation; and above all, to learn to respect the rights of each other in the post-war world as well as at the present.

Various members of this post have been delegated to attend all conferences and take the lead so as to assure them an interesting stay and to carry out real American hospitality. The discussions have been more or less informal and it is of great concern that the opinions formed by this handful were drawn from the character of the true American and not any acts of falsehood.

Our guests are leaving our humble surroundings this afternoon and we are sure that a better Anglo-American understanding has been achieved; and it goes without saying that this experiment has not been in vain.

We are in hopes that plans will materialize to have a return visit from our British Allies. We are also looking forward to the day when we may visit British units and further the interests and knowledge gained at this initial conference.

* * * * * * * * * * * * * *

It is good to know your Military Courtesy, but it is much more important to practice it.

On leave in Liverpool, 1943

From the *Bars and Stripes*, *The Unit News*, July, 1943

Young boys of wartime Liverpool, 1943

Lloyd Edison and Ellie Knaack at desk, 38th Station Hospital, Winchester, 1943

IS MY FACE RED: Miss Ray walked in on one of the Med. C ward men one morning when, accompanied by the radio, he was showing the nurses the Wisconsin version of a Jig. A Pfc. EDISON should be more dignified.

* * * *

ROVING REPORTER

FOR SALE: One slightly worn Zoot Suit, four foot chain, and hat with 5 inch brim and brightly colored band; guaranteed not to fit. A Zoot Suit never does. Any reasonable offer will be accepted. Shirt & tie will be thrown in free of charge to any fool who snatches this rare bargain. Inquire at P. X. Zoot Suit Ollinger will handle the transaction

* * * *

SUICIDE ACT: What certain nurse grabs bottles (for her cough) in the dark regardless of their content. We suggest neon lights as an aid in distinguishing the difference between Terpin Hydrate and Thawpit (a cleaning fluid) P.S. Her cough is better!

* * * *

We request that the Kitchen Mechanics stop dishing out Alphabet Soup. McKee talks enough now!

* * * *

What G.I. attends the town cinema armed to the teeth with a package of Zu Zus and a V-mail blank? He writes to his girl (with the aid of his flashlight) during the more romantic scenes and annoys the other movie-goers by crunching on the cookies.

* * * *

WISHFUL THINKING: The best method of getting a guy up for reveille is by having fresh eggs for every breakfast!!!

From the *Bars and Stripes*, *The Unit News*, July, 1943

This Tech. Sgt. was a patient in our hosp. and a very nice chap. I remarked one morning that this was the best Hosp. in the E.T.O. and one hour later I found this on the bulletin board of Medical Service. Cute, eh?

Ving.
Sept. 12, 1943

September 13, 1943

This evening finds me on C.Q. duty again, so I have a good chance of getting my correspondence up to date. This is certainly a beautiful night. The weather is clear, warm, and there's a nice big full moon. These are the kind of nights we like—nice for the blackouts but kind of bad for the air alerts. However, we haven't had any for a long time. The news of Italy certainly was good, eh? Makes us all feel six months closer to home. I'm sitting here in the recreation room, and there's hardly anyone around. There is a dance in town and many went to that. Then, too, we have a double feature movie in the auditorium and quite a few will be in there. So, I have an American program on the radio and am taking things easy. Feels good, as I have been busy for the past several days.

October 31, 1943

Was glad to hear from you and was surprised to hear of the snow you folks had in Detroit already. For some reason or other it just seemed unusual, but I guess my thinking so is due to the fact that I've only seen snow three times since I left home—once in Texas on Mt. Franklin, once in the mountains of Scotland and once here on our base. It does seem peculiar seeing so little of it in almost two years. This past week I have been keeping busy with some photography. This has been a quiet Sunday. Actually we were paid today. It is now 7 p.m. and the boys are in town and also here in the recreation room doing some gambling. Tsk, tsk, ha. Oh, I almost forgot, this is Halloween. Well, I'm all dressed in my "guess who suit" and ready to go.

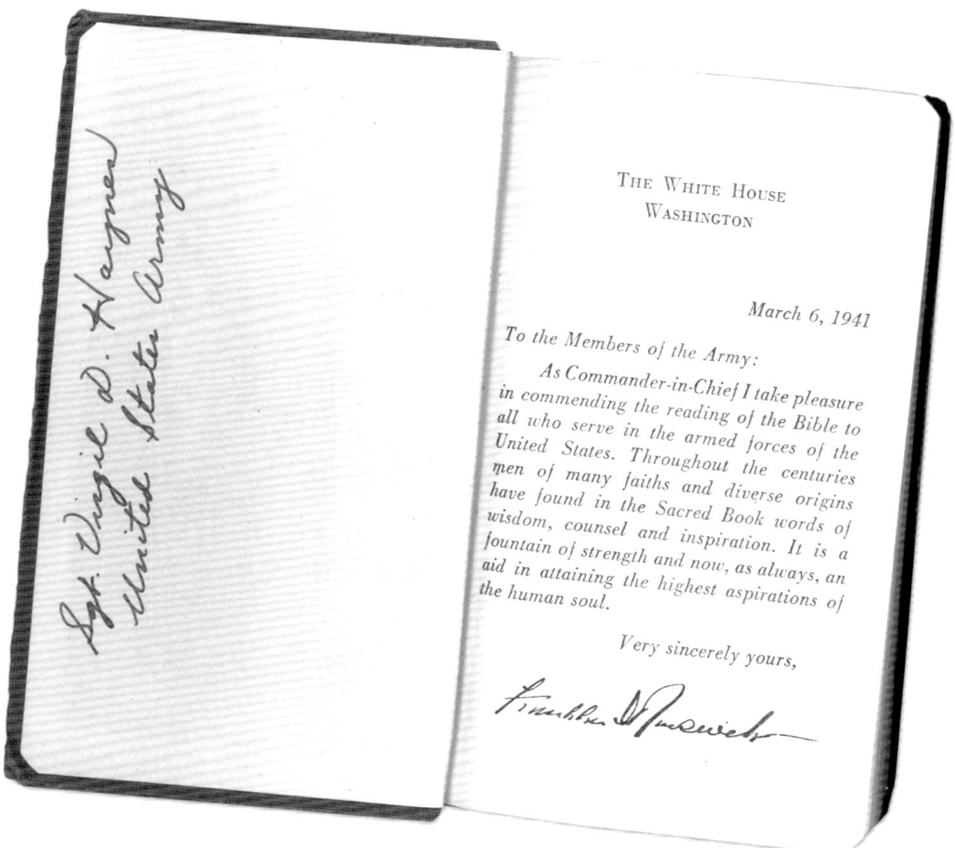

Best of wishes
from Merrie Ole England again.

A Hearty Christmas
Greeting

To forget all sadness
To remember all joys of the past
With anticipations of
much happiness
Is my wish for
Christmastide

Lovingly from

Your soldier boy.

Christmas 1943. Virgil

April 18, 1944

I'm going to try and write just a few lines before I go to bed. I just returned from a bike ride and the clock is striking ten, and that is the reason I'm tired. I've received lots of letters and V-mails, and thank you for sending the church bulletin. The music program sounded like it was very nice. Gosh, it seems strange to read a lot of new names that I don't know at the Church of the Brethren. So you are hearing about the coming invasion. Well, so do we but not in the same way you folks do back home. I know that you may be fed a lot of nonsense so don't believe it all. We are and will be perfectly O.K. Don't let the radio and newspapers upset you any. All's well and everything is fine.

April 23, 1944

Another Sat. eve and it sure is a beautiful one. We have had a perfect summerlike day, and here it is eight p.m. and the sun is still up nice and bright. As I sit here to write, I can hear some of the patients calling out the numbers for "bingo." It recalls the time when I played at the El Paso USO and almost won a telephone call home. You asked in your last letter if viewing the autopsy was compulsory. No, it wasn't, and the Army does a lot of them. So it would have laid you out, eh? It didn't bother me a bit.

April 25, 1944

'Tis almost 10 p.m. and Sgt. Hull, Sgt. Reneau and I just returned on our bikes from a picture-taking ride. The late evening sun really gives us beautiful light, so we are taking advantage of it. I think we are getting some nice pictures, too. We just got a new Cpl. in our unit by the name of George Hovey, and he comes from Harbor Springs. His dad has the drugstore there, and he knows your relatives. The first thing I said to him when he said he was from an area of northern Michigan that we know so well was, "Let's take the station wagon and drive the shore to Cross Village." It really took him by surprise! He was certainly surprised, too, that my wife happened to be born in his hometown.

I titled this one "Future Briton." I like it a lot. It is typically English, as you can see. I happened along by the school one day just as classes were dismissed, and I saw I had a picture, so I snapped... and got this. The lighting here is nice, I think.
Winchester, 1944

April 30, 1944

Well, we have been overseas for a full eighteen months, and, of course, we would like very much to get home for awhile. However, that seems to be a little out of the question at the present time. It really doesn't seem as though we have been gone from the States this long. It was such a pretty Sunday morning with the early sunshine and the crisp weather. Since we have been stationed here, I have found I like the way mornings are on the edge of a small town, and the more I see of them, the more I think how nice they would be in a place like Harbor Springs instead of a big city like Detroit. I suppose you know what I'm musing about? Could be...who knows????? As for the invasion, everyone seems to want it to get started so we can get it over with and get back that much sooner.

This afternoon I had a monthly report to get out for the Major, so I worked on that for a few hours and then went to our ball game. During the game, a P-38 fighter gave us a few buzzings, and that is certainly a beautiful ship to see overhead. It is still my all-time favorite plane as a fighter. We see lots of flights of fighters and bombers. What a sight to see and to know they are ours. Anyway, after the game we had a light supper of cold meats and salads then had an all-girl orchestra put on a show at the auditorium. Al Goodman, the popular song composer, was along and gave us a number of his new and old hits. So, all in all, I had an enjoyable day and didn't even get off the post.

This picture is of a section of tents put in place ahead of the invasion. Our Supply Sgt., Charles Smith, is from Arizona, and our Head Nurse of Medical Service, Miss Ruth Goodwin, is from Philadelphia. We have fifteen beds in each tent. They're not too bad and are very comfortable. Winchester, 1944

May 3, 1944

It was such a lovely day that Sgt. Lunceford and I went into town after dinner, since we both were able to get the same time off for a change. We did a bit of window shopping, picture taking and took in a swell show at the Ritz. We saw "Thousands Cheer" in Technicolor and also a travelogue of Niagara Falls. This, too, was in color and was very nice to see. It brought back my memories of we two there. Remember?

May 4, 1944

I was quite the artist today. I drew a number of colored drawings of various sections of the body for one of the Captains who is to give a medical talk this evening. I did all right with the job, too... I guess. Ha. I developed my latest strip of exposed film last evening. Sgt. Hull, Sgt. Reneau, Sgt. Arbaugh and I did a bit of work on our darkroom. Hope to make some prints to send you soon.

May 7, 1944

This was a very beautiful Sunday, and we had some excitement when several P-47s gave us a buzzing. The pilots had been patients here, and so they gave us a return "hello." Then tonight, a Fortress crew buzzed us, and it sure is nice to see them. Sgt. Reuter and I rushed up on top of the roof and had a grandstand view. We are going to have a Liberator crew do the same soon. Gosh, the C-47s regularly come over by the dozens. Every now and then, about a hundred fly right over our hospital, and they sure look nice. And then, all of the other planes, P-47s, P-38s, P-51s, B-17s, B-24s and lots of different kinds of British planes fly over, too. Sgt. Hull and I know about all of them because we have several airplane identification books. They sure can handle those planes well. Sometimes I wish that I had tried for the Air Corps. We even see a few German planes that have been captured and repainted and are used for training purposes. P. S. While writing this we just got buzzed by two big war-birds. They flew right by my window about fifty feet over the building. Some fun, eh?

May 10, 1944

I'm going to try and write a few lines while some prints are being washed. I just made some more contact 35mm sheets, and they came out real well. The main thing is to get some good negatives and then to enlarge them when I get home later...would you like to make it a date to help me some evening? I'm pretty tired as I've been up all night helping with some accident cases, so I guess I'll soon go get some sleep.

May 19, 1944

This morning two medical officers, three nurses and another Sgt. and I went to visit a field hospital not too far from us. Sure was interesting to see the differences between our outfit and theirs. The ride in the new Dodge ambulance was swell, and I even got to sit in front. It made me want to be home driving our little green coup with you. The highways are really jammed compared to my bike riding over them a year ago. The "Yanks" sure did invade England. Ha. We have been awfully busy getting our new medical tents in order and setting up extra wards in the hospital.

Soldiers on the move, Winchester, 1944

May 20, 1944

I've just returned from a visit to Mr. Cecil J. Blay who I had read about in the *PSA Journal*. He had written an article on photographic portfolios. I contacted him which brought me an invitation to stop by his home. They live in a pretty nice neighborhood on the edge of the city and up on a hill. It's only about a two-mile walk from the hospital and was easy to find. Mr. Blay and his wife have a five-year-old little girl, but she was to bed already, so I didn't get to meet her. But from the pictures I saw of her, she seems to be just like a five-year-old would be. They seem to be a very nice couple, and the evening was spent very well. He showed me his darkroom and many of the finer prints he has—and he certainly does have some nice ones. Most of his work is outdoor scenes, and before the evening was over, he presented me with a nice big enlargement, so, of course, I accepted it. It is a pictorial scene of a hay wagon. It is quite nice and a good job considering the subject. He sure has an awful lot of sky in it—I'll send it home to you at a later date. Mr. Blay has a number of prints hung in the salons over here and is an Associate Member of the Royal Photographic Society here in England. I was really glad I went to see him.

May 24, 1944

The clock is now almost 10 p.m.—I'm sitting here in front of an open window and looking across a nice green valley with a rolling hill loaded down with trees as a horizon. The sun is bright red, nice and round and is setting in the north by northwest. As soon as it's down, the blackout goes up. It's really peaceful here, and one wouldn't think there is a war going on, and not too far from us either.

Two peaceful views of the countryside around Winchester, 1944

"D-DAY"

6 June 1944.
England
38th Station Hosp.

My Dear Audrey,
As I start to write these lines the Bombers, Fighters and all are still going and coming - Going and coming -

Yes, this is the day we all have been waiting for, and we were all pretty much excited after we knew that the fireworks had started on the other side of the channel. Do you recall some time back about me telling you of the wonderful sight one night when we had an alert and many larger bombers all lit up like Christmas trees flew right over our hospital? Well dear, I saw that same thing early this a.m. at 2:30, and I presumed then that the invasion had started.

It was but a short time later that it was confirmed by the Headquarters of the Allied Command. We had our ears glued to the radio all day—almost. I never saw or heard so many planes in all my life as I did this morning. Then, too, we saw them return—the blue and white sky, the hundreds of bombers in the early morning sunshine—and it appeared as though every one came back according to the high numbers of planes. Some landed close to us, and how interested and excited we were!

But we had work to do and we did it. Yes, special work, and it all went A-1, and now we are waiting—just waiting patiently. We are ready and we'll give them all the best we have and then some.

Our commanding officer called a special meeting this afternoon and gave us just a word or two of the event and then turned the meeting over to the Chaplain for a word of prayer—and what a nice prayer he gave. Yes, this is a day I'll always remember. And to think that I had chicken tonight for dinner while those fellows across the water were eating K-rations in a foxhole and dodging German shells and bullets. We are ready for them and will aid them all we can.

All day long I kept thinking of you folks back in the States, and of all the excitement you must have had—radio flashes, extras and all the fanfare. Well, over here, we are keyed to the same high pitch, and we can see and hear what's going on which makes one really go sky-high.

Dear, I want to try and give you some assurance of my safety by telling you that we are O.K. with nothing to worry about. That is, hardly nothing. At the present time, me and my gas mask are the best of pals, and we will be for some time. The helmet is a handy gadget also, and that stays pretty close, too. So, all in all, if I don't worry, why should you? I'll let you know when to start, O.K.?

All my love and kisses—
hello to all— The bombers still
go over— Bye— Lovingly, Dig.

June 8, 1944

Was up last night until 2 a.m. and was busy all day today and we are getting busier. Yes, the men are coming in and we are taking care of them. We are managing all right so far. These men certainly have had some hair-raising experiences so far, and they even had the German souvenirs to prove it. They are all a pretty cheerful bunch and quite eager to get out of here and get back in the thick of the fight. I've seen and heard so many things today about front line battles, and I'll never forget them. Assure the folks that everything is O.K. This is really what we've waited and trained for over here for nineteen months—we are doing our best.

June 11, 1944

The way things are here at the hospital now, I'll have to cut out practically all my letter writing. We are really in action and "going to town" with the wounded. I really can't say what I'd like to, but speaking in soldiers' words, these fellows we are taking care of have gone through one hell of a mess, and we must give them everything possible to make it easier for everyone. These wounded soldiers are as tough as iron bars. I'm taking care of one, myself, who is full of "shot" in the hips, and his right foot is still over there in France. But what a fighter he is. For the first time since I've been on this side of the Atlantic, I slept on a Sunday afternoon. I just had to or I'd have been asleep standing up. Everyone is on call at a moment's notice, and we've experienced a 48-hour shift. We all get right to our posts and take over—it is amazing to see the co-operation and dedication to our work that we didn't even know we had. All of us medics give the wounded a lot of praise. They, in turn, give us credit and also the medical aid-men in the front lines. When we see the condition of the men coming in, it really makes us pretty mad and kind of makes us want to be over there ourselves. I'm quite sure several of our friends from back home are there, and if they are, I sure hope they come out O.K. One of the wounded German prisoners who spoke a little English said to me, "Too many Americans—too quick." So please know how busy we are and that we are all doing work that has to be done—both night and day. The operating crews are really going full blast. Everyone is pretty tired but O.K., and we shall carry on.

June 14, 1944

We are due to get real busy once again. We've had a little breathing spell, but I guess we're due to be loaded with patients again soon. We are surprised we've been going hard for this long. But, regardless of when some more wounded come in, we'll be ready. We are now getting reports of some men who died in France who we knew here in the hospital. We sure feel sorry for them. Say, don't worry about the pilotless planes. They don't bother us. Wish we would go into the invasion area. Everyone here wants to go…"Paris in the Springtime" and all that. Ha. Then perhaps into Berlin and all around.

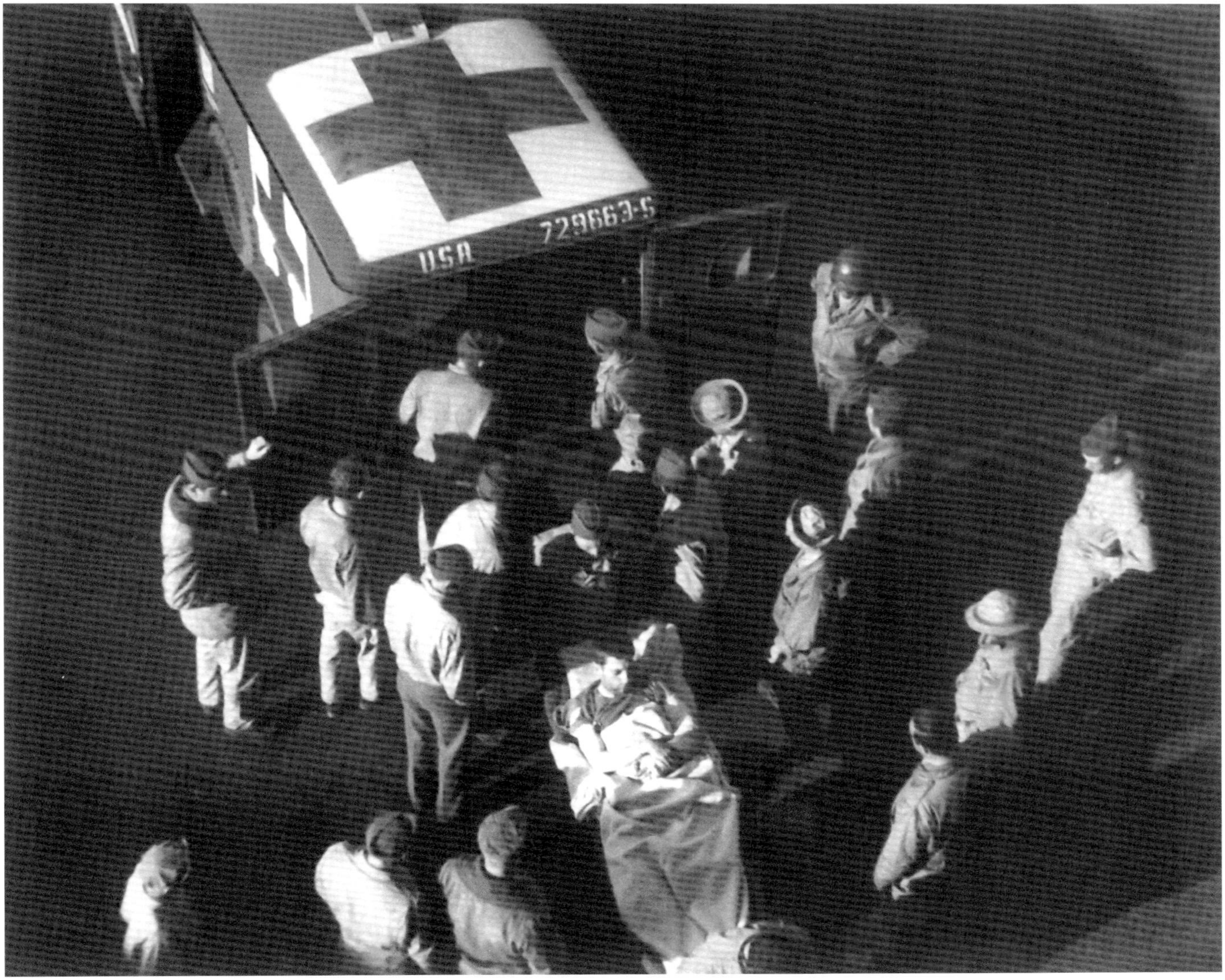

Wounded arrive at the 38th Station Hospital, Winchester, 1944

June 16, 1944

Recently, the mail has been somewhat held back—due to the invasion, I presume. One letter from you was written May 29, the same day, one year ago, that Ken lost his life on Attu, and I'm sure every one of us who knew him just kind of bowed our heads for a minute. We got some new men in our unit yesterday, and they were with a hospital unit on the island of Kiska. Two of them are assigned to me, and I have learned several things about those islands around Attu that I always wanted to know. They seem to be pretty nice fellows and are glad to be over here rather than where they were before. Another letter from you was written on D-Day. I think I know how you must have felt when you first heard the news about the invasion. So, people heard it just as I thought…in bed…and the newsboys yelling with their "extras." Well, I heard and saw it in a much different way in the early morning hours. And what a sight I saw.

It Was a Touchy Business

Doctor Removes Live Shell

A merchant seaman was brought into the 38th General Hospital in Com Z the other day. An unexploded 20mm. shell was lodged in his armpit and an operation was needed immediately.

Maj. William Denny, of Cambridge, Ohio, the hospital's chief surgeon, was called in. He asked a ballistics expert the safest method for removing the shell.

The ballistics man said that to avoid exploding the shell, he would have to keep it in a horizontal position, avoid touching it with surgical instruments, guard against jarring it or suddenly changing its position, and remove it in a backward position.

Maj. Denny listened, hesitated, and then proceeded. Partially exposing the shell with his scalpel, he discovered that a large blood vessel stretched across its base, making it impossible to follow instructions. Nevertheless, he dug deeper, beyond the shell, freed it, and carefully lifted it out in a horizontal position—unexploded.

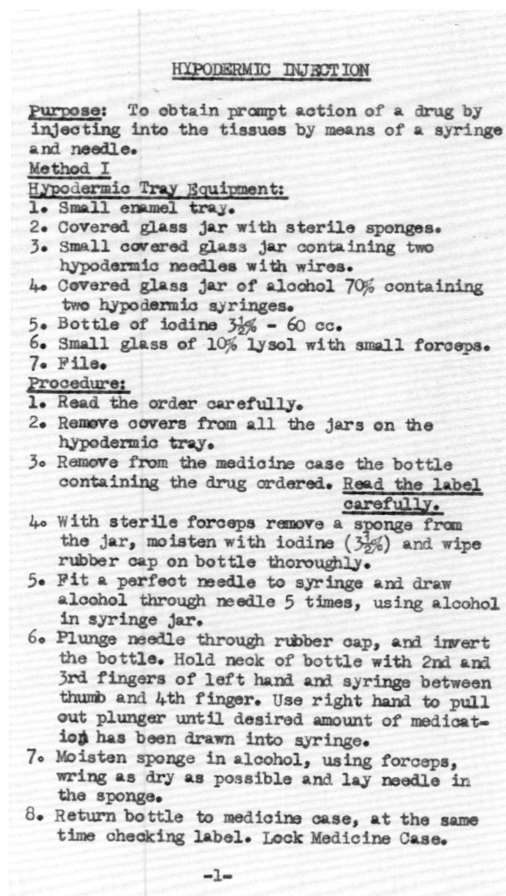

HYPODERMIC INJECTION

Purpose: To obtain prompt action of a drug by injecting into the tissues by means of a syringe and needle.

Method I

Hypodermic Tray Equipment:

1. Small enamel tray.
2. Covered glass jar with sterile sponges.
3. Small covered glass jar containing two hypodermic needles with wires.
4. Covered glass jar of alcohol 70% containing two hypodermic syringes.
5. Bottle of iodine 3½% - 60 cc.
6. Small glass of 10% lysol with small forceps.
7. File.

Procedure:

1. Read the order carefully.
2. Remove covers from all the jars on the hypodermic tray.
3. Remove from the medicine case the bottle containing the drug ordered. Read the label carefully.
4. With sterile forceps remove a sponge from the jar, moisten with iodine (3½%) and wipe rubber cap on bottle thoroughly.
5. Fit a perfect needle to syringe and draw alcohol through needle 5 times, using alcohol in syringe jar.
6. Plunge needle through rubber cap, and invert the bottle. Hold neck of bottle with 2nd and 3rd fingers of left hand and syringe between thumb and 4th finger. Use right hand to pull out plunger until desired amount of medication has been drawn into syringe.
7. Moisten sponge in alcohol, using forceps, wring as dry as possible and lay needle in the sponge.
8. Return bottle to medicine case, at the same time checking label. Lock Medicine Case.

-1-

ABOVE *From the* Stars and Stripes. *This story was suggested by Sgt. Gene Reneau but the paper called us a 'General' instead of a Station Hospital.*

RIGHT Page from The 38th Station Hospital procedural booklet.

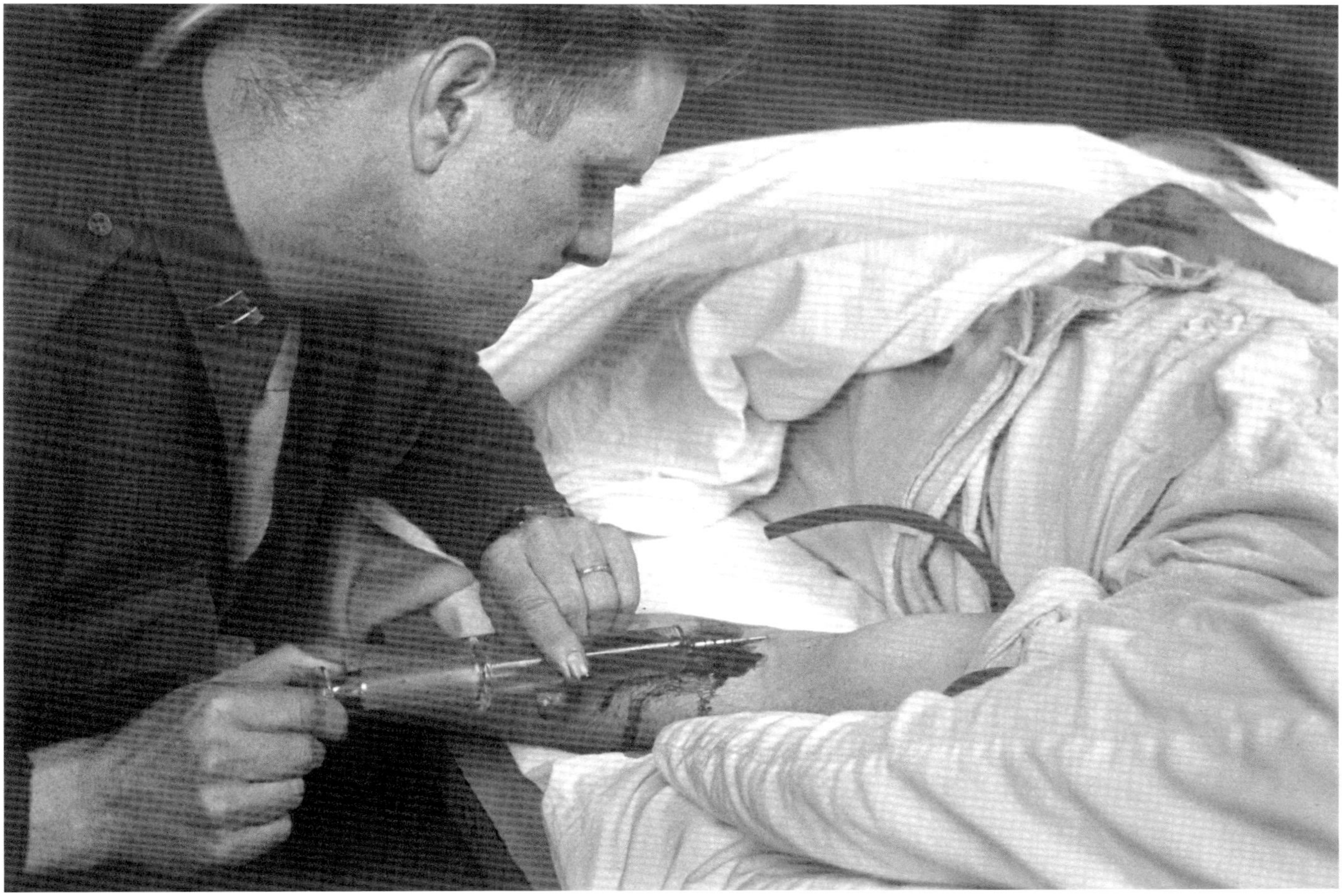

Treating the wounded at the 38th Station Hospital, Winchester, 1944

July 2, 1944

Today was the first time I was off the post since I went to visit Mr. Blay's photographic studio quite some time ago. Town is pretty empty of soldiers compared to before. Had a nice cold ham salad and some fresh strawberries for dinner. Also saw a swell movie called "Heavenly Bodies" with Hedy Lamarr and William Powell. It's pretty light out this time of year until about midnight. It's a nice cool night and I presume that I'll get a good night's sleep if the dad-gum flying bombs stay away. We can really hear them whistle and aren't exactly sure where they'll land.

July 11, 1944

We are now getting a little chance to get rested-up, and we sure do need it very much. I didn't know I could stay awake for sixty-some hours with only six hours sleep in that time. Everything's fine, we're just real tired. I actually ran across a 34-year-old chap from my old hometown of Johnstown, P.A.! He is a Miller and is related to Robert Miller and some of the others that we know back in the Haynes and Dietz homeland. He had a slight wrist wound, so we had some time to talk. I got a V-mail from my dad today. Be sure to let him know about this Pennsylvania fellow I met.

July 16, 1944

How I longed to be home today. It always seems as though Sunday is more when I think of home than any other day. I guess it did mean more to both of us than the rest of the week. I feel that before too long a time, you and I will be able to spend the day together again. If I ever complain about anything when I get home, please remind me of the things I had to put up with while away for these years. I feel now as though I've really had an important part in this war. Today, a patient needed a blood transfusion in a hurry, and so I went to the lab to have a sample taken which proved to correspond with his. Immediately, I was in the operating room giving a full pint of blood. And a short time later, a patient on one of my floors was also getting a fresh supply of blood. He has a bullet wound through his chest—a 24 year old from Mass. I keep going in to see him, and all he can say is "thank you, Sarge." The horrors of war are really starting to show up, and the more one sees of it, the more he wonders just what it's all about and why. I see from your letter that you worry some about the bombs over here. Well, as I said before, I'll be sure to let you know when to start worrying! Berlin radio reported that our English town was blown off the map. Ha. I sure can't see any part of it that was. At the moment, a band is playing the "Star Spangled Banner" in a park down below the hospital. Sounds good. The American flag flew atop the Cathedral here on the 4th of July.

Actor James Cagney visiting the wounded at the 38th Station Hospital, Winchester, 1944

July 26, 1944

I wrote you a short V-mail last night and then went right to bed. I was pretty tired as I had just returned from a trip taking two patients to another hospital quite a distance from us. This one patient was really a bad egg, and here at our hospital we had to put him in a straight-jacket to keep him out of trouble. Well, another chap and I went along with the driver. Someone always goes, but this time two of us went. Good thing we did because about half way there the patient broke away and got out of the ambulance and beat it into a swampy ravine. We finally caught him after hopping hedges, barbed wire and fences. We had to be a little stern and had quite a job getting him back, but then we had no trouble the rest of the way.

The trip was nice even though we did have that trouble. The section of England we went through is very pretty. The thing about the trip that I enjoyed most was that I drove almost 100 miles back. We had a new Dodge ambulance (made in Detroit!). It sure was a treat to drive, even on these small winding English roads where the houses stick right out in the road. Driving on the left didn't bother me a bit, and I find that I have retained my good driving qualities. Ahem! It really was nice to drive again...most of the time I made believe I was in our Chevy and you were alongside of me, and that we were buzzing through Pennsylvania as this section of England does resemble eastern P.A. Gosh, I miss our car.

Well, Sgt. Reuter has gone to the big city again. He and another soldier are going on a special "hospital broadcast" which you people will hear in the States. I guess it will be transcribed and rebroadcast. Hope you hear it. He'll be gone for a couple of days, so I'll be a little extra busy again. We all think that Germany will fall fast now, and it won't be too long until this war here is over. We sure hope we are right. It could end tomorrow and I wouldn't be mad one bit. We are all O.K.—One Happy Family! Almost anyhow.

August 3, 1944

Today Sgt. Hull and I were eating together and all of a sudden he said, "Let's play golf." So we finished eating, jumped on our bikes and played golf. It was my first time this year, and I will probably try to go some more. I enjoyed it a lot. We had a beautiful sunset, and then in a few minutes, the big, yellow full moon appeared over the downs where we were playing. It sure was nice and it felt good to be way up on top of these beautiful rolling hills.

August 11, 1944

I'll just write a few lines as we are again quite busy. We had a nice USO show in the auditorium—dancing, singing, violin solos and other entertainment. All the patients enjoyed the show a lot. Our evenings have been nice and cool, and so of course, the sleeping is A-1 except for the "doodle-bugs." We haven't really been bothered, though, for some time. Now, remember what I said about worrying—the time to worry has not come as yet. My steel helmet is right by my bed all night, and it has been worn on numerous occasions. I don't know what to say about sending me some packages for Christmas. As you know, I always will make requests for 8x10 enlarging paper, and I'm having a bad time with my watch band. But, I may be home—who knows. That trip home may be made longer by way of Japan, or perhaps India or China.

After D-Day, we did a lot of evacuating patients by way of "Hospital Trains" carrying the ever so prominent Red Crosses. We would have a short notice from Headquarters to "evacuate" and in a very short time the hospital was empty and the train fully loaded and the battle-scarred patients were off to a General Hospital miles away for better and longer treatment. All in all, it always was a thrill to go and help load, but down deep inside, one would always hate to see the load it carried. It was always a reminder that the war was on us, and that the Germans were doing this sort of butchering to our fellows. After loading, we always returned to take in a "full-house" again that just came from the boats that brought them from the Normandy beaches. So it went. Winchester, 1944

If you recall, one time not so long ago, I mentioned in one of my letters about meeting the two little gals and their family at Easton Church the time that Lloyd Edison and I went one Sunday morning. Well, now you can see that they were little. Ha. They were the nicest and most polite girls that we met over here. They just had the best personality that could be had. On Edison's left is Miss Jacqueline and on his right is Miss Jennifer. After we broke up our nice unit preparing to leave, we went out to see them for the last time and I took them a lot of things that I knew I wasn't going to use—candy, gum, games, books, etc. Well, their aunt took us to their room as they were in bed quite early. However, they were not asleep, as we heard them laughing and giggling like girls do.

Their room was a regular little gals' room and there they were, sleeping in double bunks. Well, they sure were glad to see me and especially so after I gave them all those things. They thought it was Christmas, and they certainly were happy. I even had six oranges for each one, and that is one thing they hadn't had in a long time. Well, anyhow it was fun, and I would have liked to have taken numerous other photos of them. After we left England, I received a card from each one asking me to tea. So I wrote them a letter and explained that I was unable to go. So I requested that when they visit the States, they should drop in and see us. Winchester, 1944

September 17, 1944

Well, we've left the old stomping ground, and already I miss hearing the town clock strike every hour. Our convoy trip yesterday was through some pretty scenery, and the leaves are changing color. There is a golf course near our new location that is considered one of the toughest in England. When you walk from the first hole to the 18th you have just finished almost seven miles. Yes, I said seven! Gosh, all the heather and blackberry bushes, ferns, greenery and every other thing make it rough to find a lost ball. We will go back as much as possible depending on how long we remain here. I left early this evening to sell my bike at a General Hospital nearby and got six pounds for it. The others with bikes will have to get rid of theirs, too. I am keeping my two little cameras handy and not packed away. I was able to buy a lens for my Retina that will allow me to focus on a subject only 18-inches away. Recently, I attended a beautiful little church here that dates back about 900 years. It is in a very beautiful setting. The people who live here are celebrating their "Harvest" and had all kinds of fruits, flowers, grains, etc. around on the windowsills and ledges of the church. It was quite pretty.

September 4, 1944

Evacuated all battle patients and closed the Hospital at Winchester

September 16, 1944

Left Winchester by 6×6 truck

Arrived at Camford School, near Wimbourne

October 1, 1944

Left Camford School for Bushfield

October 4, 1944

Left Bushfield Camp and boarded ship "Lady of Mann" at Southampton

Bushfield Camp staging area, England, 1944

October 4, 1944

Sailed for France—had to stay on ship four days due to storm.

October 8, 1944

Left the ship - Went ashore by L.C.T. (Landing Craft Tank)

October 8, 1944

Landed on Utah Beach - Marched seven miles inland to a cow pasture and stayed there in our pup tents.

October 14, 1944

Left for Chartres, France by ambulance (advanced group)

October 19, 1944

New hospital at Chartres

This is a bridge that was quickly rebuilt by American engineers. France, 1944

October 10, 1944

Here comes my first letter since our landing in France. Yes, it's France. Of course, we were not able to mention anything about our move. We are in the field and in our pup tents. I took a bath this afternoon out of my helmet. Since we have been here, all we have had is rain and mud. Those G.I.s that had to fight in this mud really had things tough. We have passed through several villages and have seen numerous damaged buildings. This section of France is very nice and fertile. Our first night here after a seven-mile hike in from the beach, was spent in an apple orchard. Oh, and we have hot meals, too, including white bread—the first since we left the States.

October 16, 1944

We are in our new location and buildings, and they are really "sumpin." Last Saturday, fifty of us came to our new spot. We drove in our ambulance and had a nice little convoy all the way. We came through St. Lo and numerous other cities and villages that were so smashed and battered that you couldn't see one house or building intact. I suppose you saw newsreels of St. Lo…well, they can't begin to show the half of the damage. The French might just as well forget about rebuilding that place. The muddy Normandy roads are so sloppy—just like the streets in Detroit in the winter when all the ice and snow melts into that sloppy slush. I've seen fields of our gliders from D-Day all smashed, burned and ruined, and crashed planes and burned-out tanks, trucks and all kinds of vehicles all smashed and upside down in the ditches. Seeing all these things sure is an eye-opener and makes one stop and think of the ruins and devastations of war. The further into the country we went, the nicer it got, and the city we are in has much less destruction. It's nice, and is about the same size as the one we left in England. There's a large cathedral here, and I understand it's one of the most well-known in France. I really want to walk into the center of town and see and photograph the place.

Saint-Lo in ruins, France, 1944

October 22, 1944

We've been very busy getting settled in our two new buildings. We are on the main street and right in town. I'd say that things are not quite as nice as what we had in England, but then supplies and equipment are much harder to obtain here in France as every important item is going to the front. The "Yanks" did capture a big warehouse full of German articles, and we got twelve brand new table-top radios from it. I have listened, already, to shortwave Station WBOS in Boston—direct. Our water and coal is acute, and so the hot showers and warm fires are pretty much out of the question for now. My foot locker along with all of our medical office records from our department has become lost—even our photographic printing equipment including Sgt. Reneau's negatives. By chance, I took my negatives out at the last minute and kept them with me. I'm very glad for that. We are starting to get regular mail again. By the way, I'm sorry to hear you're having difficulty obtaining a decent watch band to send me. Any old thing will do. You know the flexible band I had so much trouble with? Well, as our ship left the shores of England, I heaved one section of it in the channel, and then as we anchored off the French coast, in went the other section. So, now I feel much better about the whole thing.

November 3, 1944

We are fairly settled now, and it does make a difference. Four G.I.s went off to town this afternoon and came back with electric irons and electric heaters. So, it seems that some things are easier to obtain here than in England. Our weather's been a bit better, and it will feel good to chase the chill out of the air. I was sorry to hear of you needing to get some teeth fixed. The price sounds a bit stiff. You should be in the Army—then it would be free. The bad thing about being in the Army is that they can't supply me with free hair—Ha. Oh well, who wants any hair anyhow—not me! So you now have three boxes on their way to me. So far, none have caught up with me, but I presume they will soon. I'll be looking for that 100 ft. of film you're sending.

The back of the 38th Station Hospital, Chartres, 1944

This is a celebration of some kind in regards to a saint. I rather like this one a lot for the subjects in the foreground. Chartres, 1944

Thanksgiving, November 23, 1944

I'm listening to Churchill on the radio…I think the last time I heard him was in London last Feb., the night I ended up in that heavy German raid. He is speaking tonight on the observance of "America's Thanksgiving." We were not too busy today, and I went to our Thanksgiving service this a.m. Then, at dinner time, we really had a swell TURKEY DINNER. It was our THIRD ONE over here, too, and our memories went back to the first one where we thought and said that certainly we'd be home for the next one. Ha—were we ever fooled. I guess I should say we were just trying to keep up our morale. Well, I still have a lot to be thankful for. Since D-Day, I've been more thankful that I still have this arm and hand to be able to pen this letter to you. I've seen some who don't have this privilege now. Packages from home are starting to come in, but it looks like I'll have to wait a bit longer for mine. I don't mind waiting since the combat troops on the front lines are getting theirs first, and that's the way it should be. The only thing in the mail room for me was a letter from Mr. Blay, the photographer I visited in England. I wrote him, and they were quite pleased to hear from me and presumed I had been moved. I sent their little daughter some sticks of chewing gum in my letter, and her mother even wrote a special note and said how the little girl exclaimed, "Gee, now I can be a real Yank!"

Here's me bringing home the bacon! I mean bread.
Wish I could carry some of this bread home for you.
Sgt. Reneau snapped this on my camera. Chartres, 1944

A slow climb on snowy steps to the Chartres Cathedral, 1944

24 December 1944
38th Station Hospital
APO-517 c/o P.M.N.Y.C
U.S. Army in France.

Christmas Eve. !

Darling Audrey,

Yes, here it is another Christmas eve and how I wish I were home this evening.

Yes, it is now over *two* (2) whole years since landing over here on this side of the drink. I'm really all out of the Christmas mood this year. Plus, we've had some pretty gray and foggy weather which makes it hard for the Air Corps. But, yesterday I felt better about the whole thing because we had a party for the French children. I went over and said, "Bonjour" to a little gal and her brother. I had fun trying to speak French with them. The little girl would try so hard to understand, but a laugh ended up telling the story. She was real blonde, had blue eyes and the prettiest eyelashes. Her clothes looked a bit on the poor side, so I presume her folks weren't too rich, but she sure had a big smile all the time. We had a big Christmas tree and all the trimmings. An American Army Chaplain who spoke French did tricks for the kiddies. Then Santa gave the children their gifts. I had contributed some candies along with some paint sets that I bought in town. I guess they all had a swell time since they seemed quite happy.

Last Friday, Sgt. Reneau went to a city just outside Paris and bought a tripod, some filters, enlarging papers and a nice lens hood for my Retina. Everything seems to be available up there. Well, the weather's cleared a bit and the big moon these past few nights is very pretty, though we don't get a view of it the way we did on that beautiful hill outside of town in England.

How do you like this for backlighting? I took this on what appeared to me to be a very interesting yet typical street. Chartres, 1945

Nuns and shadows, Chartres, 1945

January 7, 1945

I'm here in my room along with Sgt. Hull and Sgt. Lunceford. We have a nice warm fire in the stove, and we are just chatting and munching on some of our Christmas goodies. It does seem queer to have to write "1945." When I left home in '42, I never thought I'd have to write '45, especially while still being in the Army. I have been a very busy chap as I am getting our yearly reports together in the form of graphs and typing. It is a big job. The deadline on it is the 10th, and I'm going full blast on it. I am even making five photo enlargements I took of our hospital building in England, and the prints will go into Washington along with the reports. I'm going to charge the unit a dollar for each. I went into town yesterday afternoon. I took several pictures and went to the marketplace which is where you can buy film, silks and everything you couldn't buy in England. Some fellows there wanted to buy my Agfa for 7,000 francs. It sure is a high price for it and yet a low one as the franc isn't worth much at the present time. I would be getting about $140.00, and in England, I paid 8 pounds or $32.00 for it. I didn't sell. You see, I'm using that camera for an enlarger, and, still I can undo it and use it for black and white pictures. The other night Sgt. Hull and I gave some lessons in photography to a Cpl. Tedder as he is quite interested in it. He is from Long Island in the summertime and St. Augustine, Florida, in the winter. Remember driving through there in early '42 and how nice we thought it was? I saw a newsreel here, recently with one of our shows, and in it was our cathedral here. It showed the fighting that went on here. Perhaps you'll see it in the States. I sent you a photo just about like in the newsreel. It was kind of a thrill to see the same scene up on the screen. By the way, how do you like the Russian advances? The POWs sure watch me mark-up the progress of our fighting forces on my large wall map at the hospital.

January 22, 1945

I was off duty all day yesterday and got a pass to stay at the Red Cross at Versailles. After a nice drive through the country which was covered with snow, I got to my destination. I joined up with a tour of the famous Versailles Palace led by a French woman who spoke very excellent English since she holds a Master of Arts Degree from Oxford. It is such a large place, and the rooms are mammoth. They were all finished in beautiful paintings, but on the invasion by the Germans, were removed by the French and most of them shipped to the States. They are gradually being returned, and some rooms are pretty well complete except for the furniture, rugs and carpets. The Chapel is truly a work of art. Perhaps you recall reading a story in the papers a short time ago about General Eisenhower's Sgt. getting married here. The Hall of Mirrors was not destroyed by the Germans. Since they had to sign the treaty there the last time, Hitler always said that it would be reversed this time, and he would sign the treaty there only on the other side of the room. But I think he'll be back on the same side as the Germans were before. Then, I looked up some photographic shops and they really have a lot of equipment in their stores. I bought 8x10 enlarging paper and a 35mm enlarger and projector combined. It is French made and is really a dandy. It is so cute and tiny, I'd like to bring it home with me.

This is a funeral at the cathedral. They've just left the church and are headed for a cemetery a short distance away. The coffin is a plain old wooden one all shined up, and it is loaded on the wagon and away they go. Chartres, 1945

I took this of the cathedral but I don't recall how the low cloudy look happened...that's a mystery. Anyway, one of the spires contained German snipers when the Yanks came through here last Aug. 15 and 16. Life Magazine *featured a picture of a Yank against an iron fence shooting away at the snipers.* Chartres, 1945

February 7, 1945

I'm up a bit late tonight, and it's for a good reason. I had gone to see a movie in our auditorium and lots of newsreels and shorts. Right after the show, we got a bunch of emergency patients who had been flown from the front lines to England. But upon arriving over the Isles, the fog was too thick for them to land. They flew back across the channel and landed near us. We took care of many casualties and really have some bad ones, too. I was also informed by my Major that I was going to be doing all the electrocardiograph work in our building. I expect to be quite busy, and I think I'll like the work a lot. I'll have a darkroom and everything. I am also on a team for treatment of patients who are in shock and an emergency team who goes with the ambulances for accident runs. Plus, I have other work throughout the wards. Oh well, this is the Army.

Entrance to the 38th Station Hospital, Chartres, 1945

U.S. Army in France
1945

Darling – You've been my Valentine a long time!

See!

Detroit 1937
V. A

V A
Detroit 1938

V A
Detroit 1939

V + A
Detroit 1940

V A
Detroit 1941

V A
Detroit 1942

V
1943
1944
1945
A

England
+
France

USA
USA

I Sure hope We Can Get these Hearts back together again in 1946

Love
V.

March 8, 1945

Last Monday morning, Sgt. Reneau and I started out for the big city of Paris, and what do you know, our train was one of those double-decker affairs. We found seats on the top deck and saw wonderful scenery that reminded me of the rolling countryside of eastern Pennsylvania. It was quite a bit different from England with homes much further apart and no thatched roof cottages at all. We did see a lot of the destruction from the bombs.

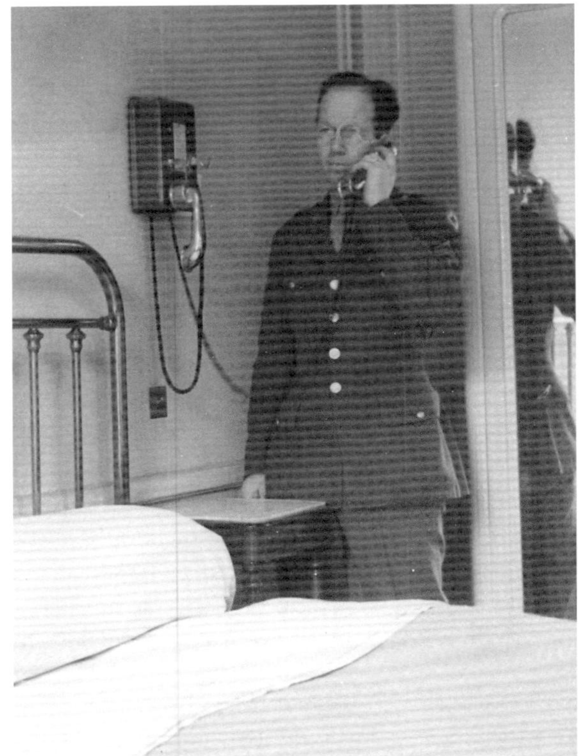

In Paris, we stayed at the Grand Central right downtown. It certainly did seem good to have a room all alone for a change. Besides a bed (with sheets, pillows and everything), I had a table, two soft easy chairs, a nice big sink and mirror and a clothes closet with a full length mirror. To top it all off, I also had the famous French telephone that one always sees in the movies, so I just had to call Reneau up several times for the fun of it. The hotel staff gave us all the service we could expect, and we sure were the big-shots for a couple of days. It was always funny to try and talk with them and to read all the French signs. We make do pretty well even though we can't speak the lingo.

The first night we were there, what a thrill to eat in a great big high-ceiling dining room with a string orchestra playing dinner music and the flags flying from all corners of the room. Yes, the American flag still looks the nicest, to me, anyhow. After dinner we went over to the Rainbow Corner (a club), and then we went to the Olympia Theater where Maj. Glenn Miller's band was playing. They sure had a crowd in there, and it is a very large and pretty theater. They put on a two-hour show plus the evening broadcast over the Forces network, and it really was swell hearing such a band, especially an American one, after not hearing any for such a long time. I could tell, though, that the ones who enjoyed it most were the chaps who got passes from the front lines, and there were a lot of them at the show. One can readily tell whether the fellows are from the "front" or the "rear," like us.

Gee, the amount of gals in Paris! And I'm referring to the WACs, the British ATS, the Red Cross gals, the French girls in the Service and numerous others. Then, when you add all the Officers, Nurses and the Enlisted Men, well, it sure does make one large crowd. The American Red Cross gals here have it pretty nice, but dear, I'd still rather have you at home than to join-up and be over here. I'll tell you more about why later when I see you. So, you remain there at home and wait for me, since I'll be along one of these fair days. It's a rugged life some of the gals have to live, and it's not for my wife. No sir.

The second day we started out on foot to do some sight-seeing and shopping. We walked the Rue de la Paix with all the stores. We also signed up for a Red Cross bus tour. We saw the Seine River with all its bridges, the palaces, Gov. buildings, Napoleon's tomb, the Louvre, the famous Eiffel Tower, the Arch De Triumph and the Unknown Soldier's Grave with its forever burning torch, the Notre Dame Cathedral and much more, but I've forgotten the names of some.

Since gasoline is a problem, there are thousands of bikes, little motor bikes and a horse and buggy is not uncommon. There is automobile traffic since some people are getting gas through the black market. There sure are some swell-looking cars running around. The hustle and bustle of people and cars is amazing. It also seems so strange to see street lights lit, too. They are not too bright, yet, but it is so much better than England where it was so black and dark.

We took in the very famous "Paris Folies" and the theater was jammed as it apparently always is. We were up in the balcony, and even though we were quite a distance away, we saw the show pretty good since I borrowed a pair of German field glasses. They came in handy. The show was all in French and consisted of songs, little plays, dances and numerous other acts. The curtains and back drops were made of so many materials and there were so many scenes, each one painted just beautiful. This is the show where the French girls dance in the nude. And they really do, too. And how. To the French this is a great art, and they think nothing of it.

OPPOSITE
Sgt. Gene Reneau in his Paris hotel room, 1945

ABOVE RIGHT
Men and women enjoy liberated Paris, 1945

March 14, 1945

It's 5 p.m. and not a thing doing, though that could change at a moment's notice. I never know how many electrocardiograms I might have to do or when. I'm writing from our new EKG room and looking out the window. Not far away are our two big cathedral spires. They sure do look pretty.

Street scene, Chartres, 1945

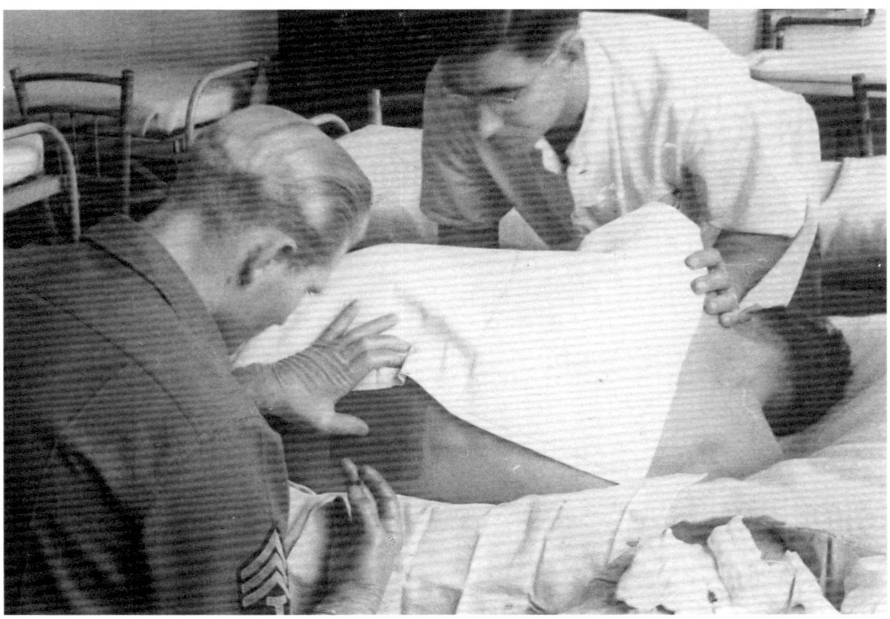

Tech. Sgts. Lloyd Edison and Hilliard "Bill" Wilson perform a procedure, 38th Station Hospital, Chartres, 1945

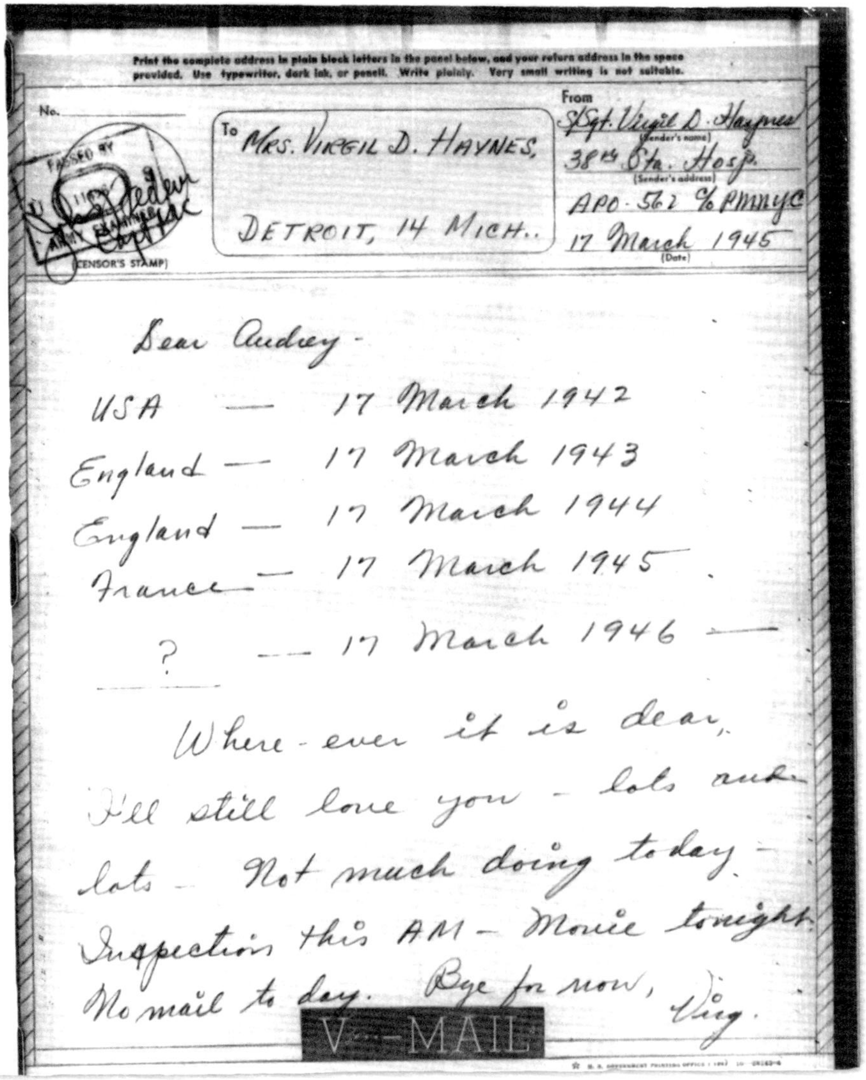

Print the complete address in plain block letters in the panel below, and your return address in the space provided. Use typewriter, dark ink, or pencil. Write plainly. Very small writing is not suitable.

No.

PASSED BY ARMY EXAMINER

CENSOR'S STAMP

To MRS. VIRGIL D. HAYNES,

DETROIT, 14 MICH..

From S/Sgt. Virgil D. Haynes (Sender's name)

38th Sta. Hosp. (Sender's address)

APO 562 % PMNYC

17 March 1945 (Date)

Dear Audrey -

USA — 17 March 1942

England — 17 March 1943

England — 17 March 1944

France — 17 March 1945.

? — 17 March 1946 —

Where-ever it is dear, I'll still love you - lots and lots - Not much doing today - Inspection this AM - Movie tonight. No mail to day. Bye for now, Virg.

V—MAIL

Easter, April 1, 1945

It seems each time one of these special days comes along, I miss being home more than any other time. I suppose it's because we always had such good times together on days such as this. I was looking forward to a nice Easter Sunday, but I was real busy this morning with our usual monthly reports. Then, too—the weather. All day it's been nasty, and we didn't see the sun at any time. I did get to church this a.m. and tried to catch the Easter message, but my mind sort of wandered back a few years to the Easter where we had the new car and we took a photo of it there in Waterworks Park. I heard some Easter music on the radio, and at dinner, I had a hard-boiled red Easter egg. That made it seem like Easter more than anything else. We sure have a lot of friends overseas in the service who are being moved around right now. It makes me look like a stay-at-home. I really do think, however, that I'll see some of the Pacific before this thing is all over, so please don't plan on me being home after we finish this end of the globe up.

April 9, 1945

Yesterday in the late afternoon, Lunceford, Reneau and I took about a five-mile hike out to the Prison Camp and back. I'm sure glad I'm on the right side of the barbed wire. We sure have a lot of prisoners, and there's plenty of room for more—as they come in they always march past our hospital. It's quite a thing to see. Well, I've had 30 months of overseas duty, now. That makes me recall how five years ago, just before we got married, I was living on Balfour with my folks, and I well remember about four o'clock in the a.m. we got a call telling us that my little niece, Norma Jean, was born. Then a short time later, the newsboys were selling their "extras" on the streets telling about the Germans going into Denmark. I didn't realize then, that five years later I'd be over here helping throw them out.

This flag picture was taken on our post April 15, the day Roosevelt died. I like this shot very much. Chartres, 1945

The river here winds through the center of town and is dirty at times and at other times quite clean. All along the river, the women do their laundry. Chartres, 1945

Parade celebrating V-E Day, Chartres, 1945

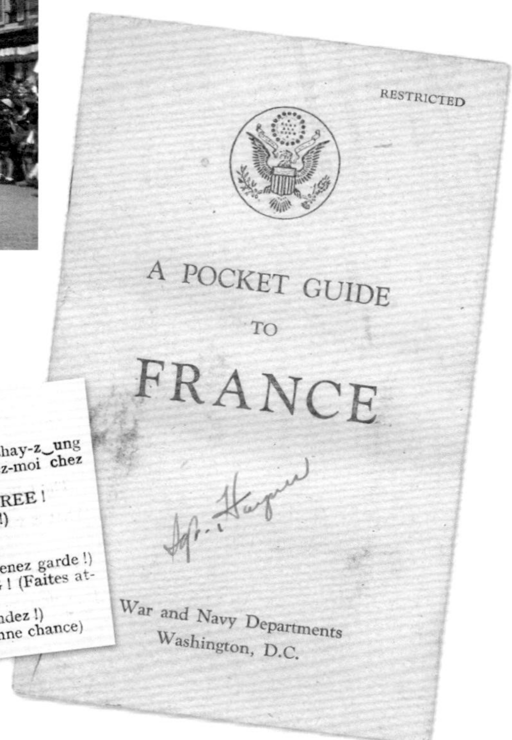

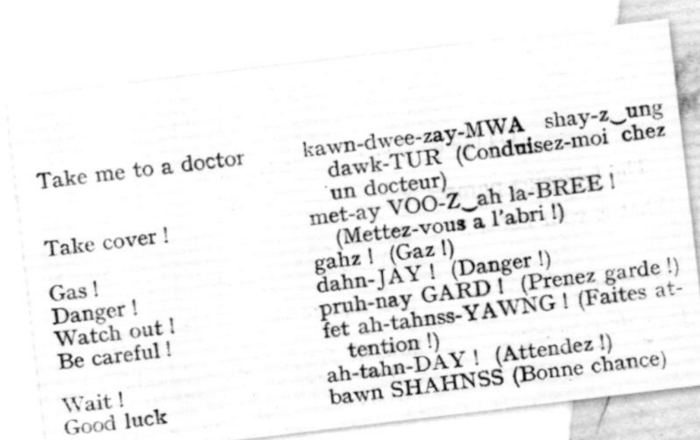

Take me to a doctor	kawn-dwee-zay-MWA shay-z‿ung dawk-TUR (Conduisez-moi chez un docteur)
Take cover !	met-ay VOO-Z‿ah la-BREE ! (Mettez-vous a l'abri !)
Gas !	gahz ! (Gaz !)
Danger !	dahn-JAY ! (Danger !)
Watch out !	pruh-nay GARD ! (Prenez garde !)
Be careful !	fet ah-tahnss-YAWNG ! (Faites attention !)
Wait !	ah-tahn-DAY ! (Attendez !)
Good luck	bawn SHAHNSS (Bonne chance)

V-E Day celebration, Chartres, 1945

May 13, 1945

We're getting some nice, warm weather, and I wish that I was home on this beautiful Sunday for Mother's Day with your mother and mine. Last Thursday was a part of my celebration of V-E Day. Four of us fellows went to St. Cloud and played golf at a very ritzy place. I suppose our troops up in Germany are really happy today. We had a three-day celebration here in Chartres (nice we can write our location now, eh?) as did the rest of France. The "Yanks" really blew the lid off of things all over.

Lady golfer at St. Cloud, 1945

Clubhouse at the St. Cloud Golf Course, 1945

OPPOSITE *A crew member turning the prop as we were getting ready to "take off" from the Chartres air strip on a C-46 troop transport. Note the cathedral in the distance. I like this shot as much as any I took.* Chartres, 1945

June 24, 1945

My furlough has ended, but I have many new experiences to remember. It was wonderful to go to Nice and to be almost like a civilian again for a few days. I want to tell you more about the trip than what I wrote to you on my postcards. We flew down in a large C-46 troop transport, and we only had about eight passengers and a crew of four. Those "46s" certainly are big planes, and it is very easy to see how they can carry vehicles and large amounts of freight and cargo. We flew at 10,000 feet and at around 180 miles per hour. The country below was like patchwork and very pretty to see in all various colors and the rivers and streams all wound around here and there. Passing over the French Alps, some of the peaks came right up to meet us. Gosh, I could have bounced a golf ball or two off some. We flew close to snow-capped mountains some with small French villages nestled at the base.

View from the C-46 troop transport over the Alps, France, 1945

One of the many planes on the sandy airstrip near Nice, 1945

Night scene in Nice, 1945

Beach bathers along the Mediterranean in Nice, 1945

Since the mountains come right down to the sea, we had to drop our altitude very fast. All of a sudden, there ahead of us was the Mediterranean Sea. What a sight that nice blue and green water was! We flew low and banked sharply over Marseille, then along the coast to a new airstrip the Army built near Nice, right on the edge of the sea.

We were assigned to the Hotel Hermitage high up on a hill overlooking the city. We ate in the big dining room, served by French waiters and had music by a French band. Through the open windows the palms swayed back and forth against a very blue sky. We fellows thought it was quite swanky. We had various day trips like to Monte Carlo, walks, bike rides, swimming, dances and shows, and it was all very entertaining.

We inquired about golf and found that it was only a nine hole course—also as the Germans left, they blew it all full of holes so it was in rather bad shape. Almost everyone speaks English because an enormous amount of tourists from England and America go to Nice in peace time. The French girls here in the South are the prettiest I've seen since leaving the States. They all wear the nicest clothes and are spic and span and natural—they don't overdo their make-up like the Paris gals.

We left Nice and flew about the same route back as we flew down. We had to circle and circle over the sea to gain our proper altitude to get over the mountains. It seemed like we were just hanging there in the wide open sky. I really liked it a lot. Also, on our way back, the pilot flew real low over the fields—like at about 50 feet—then zoomed almost straight up, and what a feeling that made in your stomach, or I should say, where it was supposed to be. Ha. He did it just for fun, and it sure was.

June 25, 1945

I'll write a few lines this evening and then it won't be too long before I'll be in bed. At the present time we're not too busy at the hospital. I suppose it will remain this way for some time. I'm getting caught up on a lot of photography, and that keeps me occupied in my spare time. I have some from my trip to Nice that I want to print.

As for my furlough home, well, that is something that flies away in the wind. All I'm doing is living by the day and wondering what will happen next. I might be in line to go to the CBI (China, Burma, India) direction.

I had a letter from Frank who wrote from Austria. He mentioned that it seemed pretty nice to walk down the street without the "Krauts" throwing the kitchen stove at them. He, too, is "sweating out" the CBI like me. I'm afraid he'll see it also.

Oh yes, he did say that (as I suspected) he came through Chartres last August 15th—he wrote that he and the others came in the front door as the "Krauts" left by the back door. And by the way, at that time when the Germans had to leave Chartres in a hurry, they went the shortest and fastest way out of town. They found they couldn't get their equipment through a beautiful old arch that spanned the river. So…BOOM…and that was that. No more arch.

A bombed-out sailing ship, Nice, 1945

Tending to the nets in Nice, 1945

945 THE STARS AND STRIP

ETO Medics Head for the Pacific

U.S. Army Signal Corps Photo

Pacific-bound medics of an ambulance company lug their gear up the gangplank of a troopship that will take them from Marseille to the Pacific. S/Sgt. Frank Jormandy of Indianapolis (left) carries his unit's administrative papers in the box under his arm. Following him is Sgt. William Grosch of St. Louis, a section leader.

Marseille Ready to Tackle Biggest Job in Long History

MARSEILLE, June 26.—France's largest port here has recovered from the Germans' masterpiece of demolition to begin the greatest job of its 2,500 years of history—that of dispatching American troops and equipment directly to the Pacific Theater.

Already several thousand service troops have sailed from Marseille to the Far East, where ... will prepare bases for the

June 27, 1945

It's very much different here at the hospital with so many men having shipped out. Our staff is really cut down, and I hope some new men come in soon—we surely can use them. My friend, Sgt. Chiapelli, really got a good set-up in his new duty at a General Hospital near Le Havre. I was sorry to lose him. He's a top-notch man. It is functioning with all German doctors, nurses and enlisted men. All the Americans have to do is supervise the whole works. I understand that this German staff has everything given to them in the best POW form possible. As for many others who have moved from Chartres, I haven't heard how they made out. It all depends on luck a lot of times. Due to our classification for Pacific duty, I'm sure hoping for that trip through the States on the way. And according to what I read in the "Stars and Stripes," we have a high priority for travel. I sure hope it's through Le Havre instead of Marseille.

OPPOSITE Exhibition of "crimes hitleriens" in Paris, 1945

crimes
hitleriens

July 4, 1945

Had a nice trip back to Paris, recently. Met up with some fellows there, and we wanted to go up the Eiffel Tower which is open again, now. Right under the Tower, the Air Force is putting an exhibit together of many popular planes, gliders and other equipment that survived Luftwaffe attacks. We all took pictures all day—along the river and even of the small "Statue of Liberty" that is on a bridge. We saw paintings and sculptures which have been returned to the Louvre and are on display again. We had a real nice couple of days.

Back in Chartres, the four of us that went to Paris—"Dudley," "Duff," Reneau and I—had a "jolly good" bull session, and then Hull and I short-sheeted "Duff's" bed. Looking back on all our time together, we fellows had a lot of fun in spite of our situation.

LEFT The Eiffel Tower and small Statue of Liberty along the Seine River, Paris, 1945

OPPOSITE Steps to the Seine, Paris, 1945

G.I. viewing the river Seine from the Eiffel Tower, Paris, 1945

July 23, 1945

There still isn't hardly anything doing at the hospital, and the rumors are flying plenty…we are going direct to Belgium, we'll be closed by the 15th, we are getting 30 days at home before the Pacific, we are going here, we are going there…all I can say is "NUTS." So, I am sorting some photographic things. I tried enlarging some of my 35mm to 9x12 prints and I was pretty much surprised that they came out as well as they did. I also made some dandy 11½x15½ enlargements and am putting these all around my room—the Eagles Wrath, the Eiffel Tower and others.

I also meant to tell you that two of the snaps of the many I sent you of the beach in Nice may not be fit to show everyone. The people in the States just look at all this nudeness entirely different than the French.

One of several military planes on exhibit, Paris, 1945

July 27, 1945

I was back to Paris yesterday. I went by myself at 9 a.m. with one of our ambulances and came back on the 8:30 train. I just went to snap some pictures and see some things I hadn't seen yet.

Our patient status at the hospital is way low so I am giving all the men lots of time off. I just went to the "Coke-bar" and got two bottles so we fellows have been sipping cold Cokes all day in our room. I'm enclosing an article from the *Stars and Stripes* and, of course, I had to take a "razzing" of the story about Detroit. In fact, the fellows put one like it on my wall locker with a cartoon they made up. It's pretty good. We are always playing pranks on each other. It's all good clean fun, anyhow.

Place de la Concorde, Paris, 1945

Detroit Manhood Swears It Wears No Girl's Panties

DETROIT, July 21 (ANS).—It just couldn't happen in Detroit. It just couldn't. And if it could who was going to show off the evidence.

That was the attitude in this Michigan stronghold of manhood today when City Fathers learned of a charge that male Detroiters were wearing women's lace panties.

The allegation was made by a Detroit wholesale dry goods firm in a letter to Sen. Homer Ferguson (R.-Mich.) citing the extremity of a textile shortage in the city of much manufacturing but little men's underwear.

Mayor Edward J. Jeffries and several Councilmen headed the anti-panty group and Councilman Harry S. Sweeny even offered to doff modesty and his pants for the cause and prove it wasn't so.

But Department store buyers weren't so sure. No, they didn't have any proof but as one of them said, "every now and then a woman insists on the plainest knitted white underpants we have and in a size that wouldn't fit her."

How about this? eh?

A plane that made 75 bombing missions on exhibit under the Eiffel Tower, Paris, 1945

July 31, 1945

Well, today we started to tear-up the joint. Our living quarters floors are "no more." Tomorrow, we finish the job and in a couple of days, bye-bye for a short distance away. I'll tell you about that later. I must get a lot of my items together, yet, and I may start that tonight.

From what I've been reading and hearing, I now feel as though our chances of going to the Pacific through the U.S. are 50-50. I sure have my fingers crossed, and crossed harder than ever this time. I just have a hunch that soon I might be able to drive you on a week's vacation in that Chevy of ours. September would be a grand time to drive up into the North Woods. I don't know what will happen, but I'm prepared to pack at a minute's notice. And if I'm U.S. bound, a half minute will do. As you can see by my terrible penmanship, I'm pretty excited and you know it's only the very important items that get me excited. You keep your fingers crossed, too, dear.

August 5, 1945

Left Chartres, France for Le Mans, France
-by train-

EDITOR'S NOTE

The formal Japanese surrender, September 2, 1945, brought an end to World War II. Virgil D. Haynes' letters from the final months of his service in Europe are, as yet, undiscovered.

Le Mans Cathedral, 1945

OPPOSITE

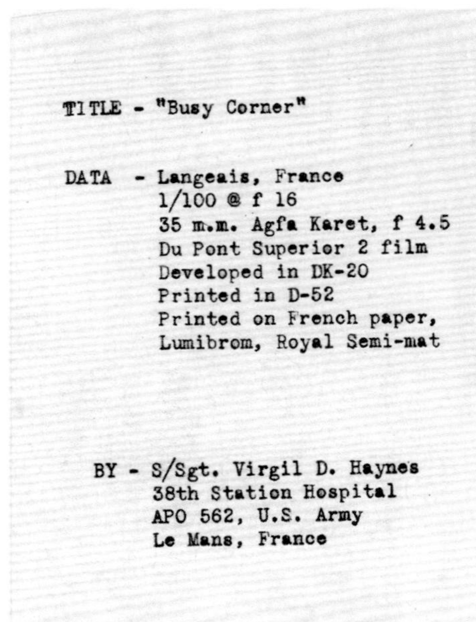

TITLE - "Busy Corner"

DATA - Langeais, France
1/100 @ f 16
35 m.m. Agfa Karet, f 4.5
Du Pont Superior 2 film
Developed in DK-20
Printed in D-52
Printed on French paper,
Lumibrom, Royal Semi-mat

BY - S/Sgt. Virgil D. Haynes
38th Station Hospital
APO 562, U.S. Army
Le Mans, France

RESTAURANT

Country road outside Le Mans, 1945

The corner "Boucherie," near Le Mans, 1945

Fishing near Le Mans, 1945

October 12, 1945

Left hospital at Le Mans for
Neufchatel-En-Bray by 6x6 truck
(Transferred from 38th Station Hospital to
Hq. 60th Medical Bn. —Stationed in an
old Chateau 20 miles southeast of Dieppe)

POW near Dieppe, 1945

Figures on a hill in the French countryside, 1945

November 6, 1945

Left Chateau near Dieppe by jeep for Camp Herbert Tareyton at Le Havre

November 11, 1945

Left Le Havre, France and boarded ship "Vassar Victory" – sailed for the U.S.

November 19, 1945

Landed in Boston Harbor and to Camp Miles Standish

November 21, 1945

Left Camp Miles Standish by troop train

November 23, 1945

Arrived Fort Sheridan, Ill. near Chicago

November 24, 1945

Discharge from Army – Fort Sheridan

November 25, 1945

Met Audrey – Rockford, Michigan

November 28, 1945

Arrived in Detroit

Homeward bound on the "Vassar Victory" somewhere in the Atlantic, November, 1945

A delayed-shutter self-portrait of Virgil D. and Audrey Haynes in 1942 which Audrey kept on her night table throughout the years in which Virgil was overseas.

END-OF-WAR LETTER EXCERPTS

FROM AUDREY HAYNES IN DETROIT, MICHIGAN TO VIRGIL D. HAYNES

August 14, 1945

Hello, darling. This will be a long day but a happy one. I awoke at about 6 a.m. when the people next door received a telephone call. With all the windows opened, I could hear, as their dining room is next to my bedroom. I heard her say, "The war's over? That's swell," so I was out of bed in a flash. I called Mother, but they were listening to the radio already. Then I called your folks and got your sister, Marian, out of bed. I'm keeping close to the radio today, and I'm excited.

August 15, 1945

This is what we've been waiting for, dear, and I know you're as glad as I am that very soon the guns will be stopped and the lights will go on again all over the world. I listened to the radio yesterday from 6 a.m. to 7 p.m. My hopes went up and down as they announced they had the peace note and that they didn't have it. Then finally at 7 p.m.—Flash!!! "The Japs have accepted the allies' peace terms." That was music to my ears. I bought an "Extra" newspaper to keep for you. I breathed a little prayer that you'd get home soon and was thankful you wouldn't have to go to the Pacific. I, on the other hand, couldn't help but feel sorry for people we know like the Gordons and the Englands who lost loved ones. We *have* paid a high price for peace.

November 11, 1945

I just received your V-mail of October 31. You sounded a bit encouraged about your place in the "coming home" schedule. Gee, four Halloweens overseas and still the same costume—a G.I. Yank! The news is listing all the troops coming in from Le Havre, and there sure are a lot of them. I feel sure you'll be among them one of these days. I'm just waiting for that phone call. I just know I'll be so excited I'll hardly be able to talk, but that will be a happy moment, knowing you are in the States.

All my love, Aud.

P. S. We just heard the Army Hour on the radio and they had a short broadcast from Le Havre. It made me feel a little closer to you, but then I wondered, were you there or already on the high seas???

EDITOR'S NOTE

Audrey wrote over 700 letters to Virgil during his time in the service and he numbered, saved and sent home every one.

LEFT Virgil D. Haynes with his 4x5 Speed Graphic, c. 1955 (photographer unknown)

RIGHT Photography by Haynes on Main Street, Harbor Springs, Michigan, c. 1950

AFTERWORD

From an interview with Virgil D. Haynes in 1994

"When I was very young growing up in Pennsylvania, before we moved to Detroit, my Uncle Vernon Dietz took some photographs, and I thought that was interesting. In the late thirties, my brother-in-law, Robert Smith, a chemist for Henry Ford in Dearborn, saw me taking pictures with my folks' camera—a 116 with a pull-out lens. He told me that J.L. Hudson in downtown Detroit had a Voigtlander 120 for sale at twenty-two dollars and fifty cents, and that was a good price for a camera. I didn't really think about becoming a photographer—I just liked to shoot what was interesting to me. I used the Voigtlander for quite a while. It was limited, but I used it. It had a three-point-five lens, and it would go to a full one-second exposure where my mother and dad's camera only had three or four shutter speeds.

"After Audrey and I got married in 1940, we took some trips to Florida, and I shot photographs along the way. When I was sent to Europe in World War II, I had to send my camera back home from New York harbor. I wasn't allowed to have it. Once I got overseas, I picked up two 35mm cameras in England. I wanted something to do other than strictly Army activities, and was glad to be shooting photographs. The first few months I sure could have taken pictures of quite a few broken collarbones that the G.I.s had because no one was used to the different front wheel brakes on the English bicycles.

"The Red Cross had a photographic contest in '43 in London—it was a big contest. I won a prize for my shot of a soldier silhouetted against Winchester Cathedral. I still have the five-dollar war bond I won, and the photo was published later in the July 1944 edition of *Popular Photography*. This gave four of us buddies in our outfit the idea to print our own pictures, so we started using the x-ray department in our hospital unit. After D-Day, lying on my bunk one day in France, I started thinking about maybe opening my own studio once I got home.

"After the war, I attended the Detroit School of Photography and thought I'd end up working in Detroit. I also ordered a 4x5 Speed Graphic. G.I.s were allowed to order the first of those cameras made after the war. In the meantime, Audrey's relatives up north in Harbor Springs kept convincing us we should move there. They even found us a place to live. So in '46, we moved into what we called the 'little house on Hoyt,' and I opened Haynes Studio. I put a gallery and studio in the biggest bedroom and developed my film in the bathtub. By 1947, we bought the Main Street store and apartment and called our business Photography by Haynes which Audrey and I operated for 28 years in Harbor Springs."

EDITOR'S NOTE

This interview was with Cynthia A. Haynes in preparation for a special photographic exhibit.